The MAILBOX®

Almost Ready to Read

Fun-filled **activities** and **reproducibles** for building
early literacy skills

Phonological Awareness
rhymes • sounds • syllables

D1717153

Print Awareness

concepts of print • environmental print • book awareness

Letter Knowledge

letter recognition • letter identification • letter formation

Editorial Team: Becky S. Andrews, Randi Austin, Diane Badden, Paula Beckerman, Kimberley Bruck, Karen A. Brudnak, Kitty Campbell, Jenny Chapman, Pam Crane, Kathryn Davenport, Roxanne LaBell Dearman, Beth Deki, Lynette Dickerson, Lynn Drolet, Amy Erickson, Sarah Foreman, Kristin Bauer Ganoung, Kathy Ginn, Heather E. Graley, Tazmen Hansen, Marsha Heim, Lori Z. Henry, Lucia Kemp Henry, Jennie Jensen, Laura Johnson, Kimberly Krikorian, Debra Liverman, Coramarie Marinan, Julie McCray, Dorothy C. McKinney, Thad H. McLaurin, Janna Meister, Sharon Murphy, Jennifer Nunn, Gerri Primak, Mark Rainey, Jenny Ramsey, Greg D. Rieves, Jacinda Roberts, Hope Rodgers, Eliseo De Jesus Santos II, Donna K. Teal, Joshua Thomas, Melissa Weimer, Zane Williard

Plus
teacher-friendly
assessment tools!

www.themailbox.com

©2009 The Mailbox® Books
All rights reserved.
ISBN10 #1-56234-881-7 • ISBN13 #978-156234-881-6

Manufactured in the United States
10 9 8 7 6 5 4 3 2 1

Table of Contents

Phonological Awareness

Print Awareness

Letter Knowledge

Skills Overview

Phonological Awareness

assessment
- beginning sounds, 33
- phonemes, 34
- rhymes, 31
- syllables, 32

beginning sounds
- matching, 12, 28
- producing, 15
- recognizing, 11
- sorting, 13, 14, 15, 24, 25

ending sounds
- matching, 29
- sorting, 14

phonemes
- blending, 16, 17, 18, 19, 26
- manipulating, 19
- segmenting, 17, 18, 19, 26, 30

rhymes
- completing, 7, 20, 21, 22, 23, 24
- hearing, 5, 6, 20
- identifying, 27
- producing, 8
- supplying, 8

sentences
- hearing words, 9, 23

syllables
- hearing, 10

Print Awareness

assessment, 57–62
basic punctuation, 44
book handling, 41, 53, 54
concepts of print, 43, 44
connecting spoken and written words, 35
environmental print, 39, 40, 51, 52

letters and words
- identifying, 56
- sorting, 42, 55

names
- letters in, 35
- recognition, 36, 45
- writing, 37, 46

one-to-one word correspondence, 42
purpose of print, 37, 38, 39, 47, 48, 49, 50
tracking print, 41, 45
word spacing, 43

Letter Knowledge

assessment
- letter recognition, 93
- lowercase letters, 95
- partner letters, 96
- uppercase letters, 94

concept of letters, 63, 79
distinguishing letters, 77, 78, 87, 88
formation of letters, 64
matching letters, 65, 66, 67, 68, 80, 81, 82, 90, 91
naming letters, 72, 73, 74, 75, 76, 86, 87
partner letters, 92
recognizing letters, 69, 70, 71, 83, 84, 85, 89
sequencing letters, 71
sorting letters, 71

What's Inside

Over 80 activities!

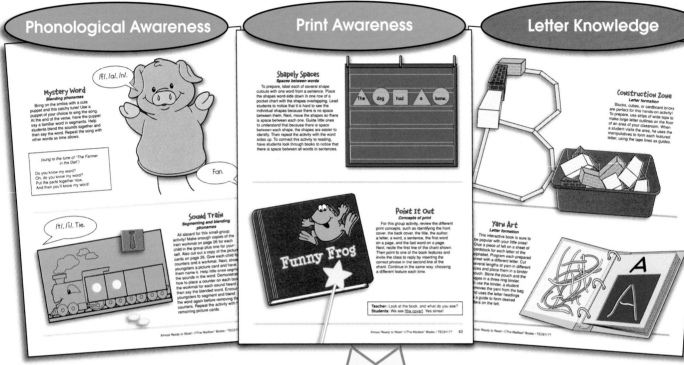

Phonological Awareness

Mystery Word
Blending phonemes

Bring on the smiles with a cute puppet and this catchy tune! Use a puppet of your choice to sing the song. At the end of the verse, have the puppet say a familiar word in segments. Help students blend the sounds together and then say the word. Repeat the song with other words as time allows.

(sung to the tune of "The Farmer in the Dell")

Do you know my word?
Oh, do you know my word?
Put the parts together now.
And then you'll know my word!

Sound Train
Segmenting and blending phonemes

All aboard for this small-group activity! Make enough copies of the train workmat on page 26 for each child in the group plus one for yourself. Also cut out a copy of the picture cards on page 26. Give each child to counters and a workmat. Next, show youngsters a picture card and have them name it. Help little ones segment the sounds in the word. Demonstrate how to place a counter on each box on the workmat for each sound heard as you say the blended word. Encourage youngsters to segment and blend the word again before removing the counters. Repeat the activity with the remaining picture cards.

Print Awareness

Shapely Spaces
Spaces between words

To prepare, label each of several shape cutouts with one word from a sentence. Place the shapes word-side down in one row of a pocket chart with the shapes overlapping. Lead students to notice that it is hard to see the individual shapes because there is no space between them. Next, move the shapes so there is space between each one. Guide little ones to understand that because there is space between each shape, the shapes are easier to identify. Then repeat the activity with the word sides up. To conclude this activity to reading, have students look through books to notice that there is space between all words in sentences.

Point It Out
Concepts of print

For this group activity, review the different print concepts, such as identifying the front cover, the back cover, the title, the author, a letter, a word, a sentence, the first word on a page, and the last word on a page. Next, recite the first line of the chant shown. Then point to one of the book features and invite the class to reply by inserting the correct phrase in the second line of the chant. Continue in the same way, choosing a different feature each time.

Teacher: Look at the book, and what do you see?
Students: We see [the cover]. Yes sirree!

Letter Knowledge

Construction Zone
Letter formation

Blocks, cubes, or cardboard bricks are perfect for this hands-on activity! To prepare, use strips of wide tape to make large letter outlines on the floor of an area of your classroom. When a student visits the area, he uses the manipulatives to form each featured letter, using the tape lines as guides.

Yarn Art
Letter formation

This interactive book is sure to be popular with your little ones! Glue a piece of felt on a sheet of cardstock for each letter of the alphabet. Program each page beginning with a different letter. Cut several lengths of yarn in different sizes and place them in a binder pouch. Store the pouch and the pages in a three-ring binder. To use the binder, a student removes the yarn from the bag and uses the letter headings as a guide to form desired letters on the left.

Almost Ready to Read • ©The Mailbox® Books • TEC61177 43

Patterns, cards, and practice pages!

PLUS

Informal assessment tools!

Monster Patterns
Use with "Read Me" on page 77.

name
takes care of books!

computer

Peanuts for Sale
Identifying letters and words

Color by the code.

Color Code
letter—blue
word—red

man	dog	r
at	s	b
f	sun	v	in

Wake Up, Farm!

A	R	W		M	T	O
B	F	Y		P	S	N
U	C	H		D	L	K
r	x	p		e	q	n
m	g	l		h	z	a
j	v	f		b	i	s

Print Awareness Recording Sheet

Name _____ Date _____

Booklet	Skills	Comments
Cover	• Front cover	
Pages 2 and 3	• Print carries the message • Where to start and stop	
Pages 4 and 5	• Left-hand page first • Letters and words	
Pages 6 and 7	• From left to right	
Pages 8 and 9	• Return sweep	

Phonological Awareness

Roll It!
Hearing rhymes

For this game, cover two empty cube-shaped tissue boxes with different colors of paper and enlarge a copy of page 20. Cut out six pairs of the rhyming pictures and glue one of each pair to a different cube, one card per side. Have little ones sit in a circle. Ask a different child to roll each cube. All youngsters say each picture word and, as a group, decide whether the two words rhyme. If the words rhyme, the students stand; say, "Rhyme time!" as they wave their arms; and then sit down. If the pictures do not rhyme, the students do nothing. Continue the game, making sure each child gets to roll a cube one or more times.

To the Market
Hearing rhymes

After a read-aloud of *To Market, To Market* by Anne Miranda, display stuffed animals, puppets, or pictures to represent some of the animals from the story (pig, hen, goose, trout, cow, lamb, duck, and goat). Then set up a market area with items or pictures of items—such as a wig, a pen, jam, a truck, and a boat—whose names rhyme with the animals' names that are displayed. Invite a volunteer to choose an animal to take "shopping." If desired, provide a toy shopping cart for the child to use. Then have him "buy" the item from the market that rhymes with the chosen animal. Ask the class to name the two items to determine whether the words rhyme. Return the items and continue the activity until each child has had a turn.

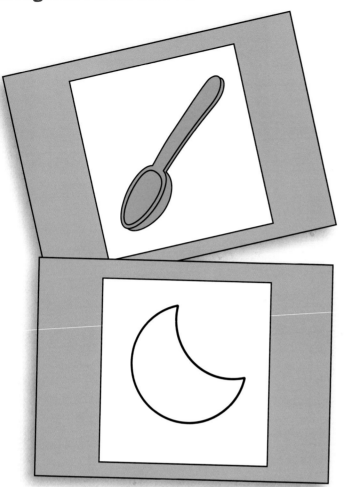

PartNer Up
Hearing rhymes

Finding a rhyming partner is the goal of this small-group activity. Copy and cut out enough rhyming pairs of the picture cards on page 20 for each child in your group to have a card. Glue each card on an index card for durability. Give each child a card and have one student name the picture on his card. Ask each youngster to repeat the name and then say the name of the picture on her card. The student who has the rhyming picture card stands and then sits next to her rhyming partner. Continue in the same manner until each child has found her partner.

Ripe for the PickiNg
Hearing rhymes

To prepare for this circle-time game, glue a copy of each picture card from page 20 to a separate apple cutout. Place the apples, picture-side down, in a pocket chart. Invite a volunteer to pick a pair of apples from the chart and turn them over. Ask little ones to name the chosen pictures and decide if the words rhyme. If they do, the child puts the apples in a basket. If they do not rhyme, she returns them to the pocket chart. Play continues until all of the rhyming pairs have been matched.

Not Me!
Completing rhymes

Have each child cut out a copy of the chair, hat, boat, and truck picture cards on page 20 and the booklet pages on pages 21 and 22. Ask little ones to follow along as you read aloud each booklet page. Pause at the end of each question and have each child glue in place the picture card that completes the rhyme. When the glue is dry, help him staple the booklet pages between construction paper covers. Then lead students in reading their booklets together.

Higgledy-Piggledy
Completing rhymes

A perky pig is just what you need to get little ones chiming in on rhymes! To make the pig, cut out a pink construction paper copy of the pattern on page 24, attach it to a craft stick, and add a small loop of tape to the mouth. Also cut out a copy of the food cards on page 23 and display the cards. To introduce the rhyme shown, say the first line, emphasizing *frapple.* In the second line, pause before *apple.* Use the stick puppet to direct the youngsters' attention to the apple card. After students name *apple* as the rhyming food, stick the card to the pig's mouth and finish the verse, emphasizing *frapple* once more. Remove the card and repeat for each remaining food card, substituting a rhyming nonsense word in the first and last lines each time.

Higgledy-Piggledy
Higgledy-piggledy [frapple]!
The pig has eaten the [apple]!
He's chewing so fast.
He's having a blast.
Higgledy-piggledy [frapple]!

Shine It
Supplying rhymes

Gather several items whose names have easily identifiable rhymes and place them in your circle-time area. (Consider a toy car, a stuffed bear, a book, a pen, a sock, and a mug.) Give one student a flashlight and turn out the lights. Recite the rhyme shown, adding at the end of the second line a familiar word that rhymes with one of the items. Continue the rhyme, and at the end of the last line, have the child holding the flashlight turn it on, shine it on the object with the rhyming name, and name the item. Pass the flashlight to another student and repeat the process until each child has had a turn.

One, two, three, turn out the light.
Which object rhymes with [star]?
One, two, three, shine your light.
The rhyme we see is [car]!

Silly Name Song
Producing rhymes

This catchy tune will get everyone involved in circle time! Demonstrate how to change the beginning sound of your name to make a new name that rhymes. Lead little ones in the song shown, inserting a consonant sound in the last line. Then go around the circle and have each child say her name and the new rhyming name that begins with the chosen beginning sound. Repeat the song and activity using a beginning sound each time.

Cindy, Bindy!

(sung to the tune of "The Muffin Man")

Oh, do you have a silly name,
A silly name, a silly name?
Oh, do you have a silly name?
Use (/b/) to make a rhyme.

Ups and Downs
Hearing words in sentences

Get everyone moving while listening to the individual words in sentences. Direct students to get into a squatting position. Announce a sentence containing the word *up* or *down.* Have students listen to the sentence for the word *up* or *down* and then either jump up or sit down accordingly.

Feeding Time!
Hearing words in sentences

Use the familiar book *The Very Hungry Caterpillar* by Eric Carle to help little ones listen for a specific word. Give each student a copy of the caterpillar card on page 23 and a bingo dauber. Read the story aloud while youngsters listen for the word *hungry*. Each time they hear the word *hungry*, they make a dot on their caterpillars' bodies. At the end of the story, lead students in counting the dots to see how hungry the caterpillar was!

El-bow

Rat-a-tat-tat,
Rat-a-tat-tat,
Point to your [elbow]
And give it a pat!

Rat-a-tat-tat!
Hearing syllables

A rhythmic chant is the perfect way to provide practice with listening for word parts! Say the chant shown and direct students to listen for the name of a body part. When they hear it, they should pat the named body part the number of times to correspond with the number of syllables. Repeat the chant several times, saying a different body part each time.

Name Game
Hearing syllables

To prepare, post cards numbered 1–4 in different locations in an open area of the classroom. (If a student has more than four syllables in her name, post the matching number as well.) Say a familiar name and lead students in clapping the syllables. Next, have each child, in turn, clap the syllables in her name. On your signal, invite each student to stand by the number that matches the number of syllables in her name. After confirming each child's placement, repeat the game using last names.

Re-bec-ca!
That's three parts!

Jar, jeep.

Hoop Hop!
Recognizing same beginning sounds

All you need for this activity is a plastic hoop or yarn circle for each child. Have each student stand behind her hoop. Announce two words, emphasizing the beginning sound of each. Have each child determine if the words begin with the same sound or not. If they begin with the same sound, each youngster hops into her hoop. If they begin with different sounds, she does nothing. Continue calling out pairs of words as time allows.

Pass the Bag
Recognizing same beginning sounds

To prepare for this circle-time activity, gather groups of small items or pictures of items whose names each begin with one of several beginning sounds; then place each set in a separate bag. Lead little ones in the song shown as they pass a closed bag around the circle. When the song ends, the child holding the bag removes an item from the bag, names it, and then places his item in front of him. Repeat the song and bag-passing until the bag is empty. Invite little ones to identify the beginning sound that all the objects share. Repeat the activity with the other bags as time allows.

(sung to the tune of "London Bridge")

Pass the bag from friend to friend,
Friend to friend, friend to friend.
When the song stops, reach right in.
What do you have?

Dear Family,
We are practicing listening to the beginning sounds in words. Please send an item to school that begins with the letter _n_ by October 13. Your item will be returned the following week.

Thank you,
Ms. Deki

All Around the Circle
Matching beginning sounds

Prior to completing this activity, assign each child a consonant sound so that pairs of students have the same sound. Then send a note home requesting that each youngster bring in an item, or a picture of an item, that begins with her assigned sound. During circle time, invite a student to display her item and name it, stressing the beginning sound. Go around the circle and have each child name her item until the matching beginning sound is discovered. Then have the twosome sit next to each other. Continue in this manner until all partners have been matched.

Take It, Name It
Matching beginning sounds

For this small-group activity, place in a bag an object for each student so there is an object with the same beginning sound as each youngster's name. Invite a child to reach into the bag, remove an object, and name it. If the object begins with the same sound as the child's name, she keeps it. If not, a child whose name does match the beginning sound of the object may claim it. Continue until each student has an object. Then go around the group and have each child say her name and the name of her object.

Maddie, mitten!

Please Feed the Animals!

Sorting beginning sounds

It's snacktime for the animals at this center! Attach a cut-out copy of each animal pattern on page 24 to a separate paper lunch bag. Also copy and cut out the last two rows of picture cards (*c* foods and *p* foods) on page 25. Place the cards and prepared bags at a center. A student names the picture on a card, emphasizing the beginning sound. Then he decides if the food begins with the same sound as *pig* or *cat* and "feeds" the card to the corresponding animal. Play continues until the child has fed all the food to the animals.

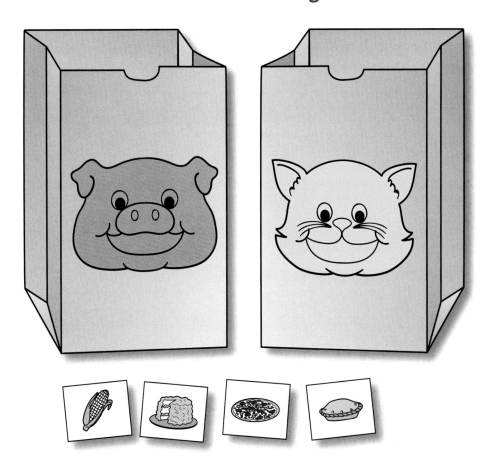

Say Cheese!

Sorting beginning sounds

Prepare a construction paper copy of the camera pattern from page 24 for each student, being sure to cut along the two dotted slits. Give each child a camera, two 3" x 12" construction paper strips (film strips), and a copy of two rows of picture cards from page 25 (photos). Have each student cut apart the cards, sort them by beginning sounds, and glue or tape each set to a separate film strip. Assist each youngster in threading his strip through his camera. As he pulls the strip, encourage him to name each picture and emphasize the beginning sound.

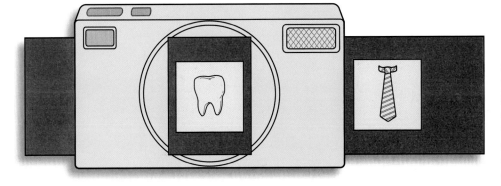

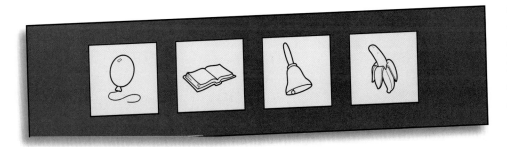

Phonological Awareness

Three-Ring Circus
Sorting beginning sounds

Come one, come all, to this small-group sorting game! In advance, cut a plastic six-pack ring lengthwise so you have two sets of three connected rings. Also cut out a copy of two rows of picture cards from page 25. Place a picture representing each sound above each set of rings. Help the group members sort the remaining cards by beginning sounds into the matching set of rings.

Sound Bins
Sorting beginning or ending sounds

For this center activity, label each of several bins or baskets with a picture representing a different beginning (or ending) sound. Place the bins at a center along with an assortment of items or pictures of items whose names begin (or end) with the same sounds as the labels on the bins. A child sorts the items into the bins with the matching sounds. Once all the items have been sorted, he checks his work by naming the picture on the bin followed by the names of the items inside.

All Aboard!
Sorting beginning sounds

Get youngsters on the right track with this sorting center. Gather four small boxes, such as shoeboxes. Cover one with black paper and add details so it resembles a train engine. Cover each of the remaining boxes with a different one of the following colors of paper: red, blue, and purple. Add paper wheels and tape the boxes together, open side up, to make a train. Copy and cut apart a set of the /r/, /b/, and /p/ picture cards on page 25. Place the cards and train at a center. A student sorts each picture card into the train car whose color has the same beginning sound. If desired, add objects with the featured beginning sounds to the center for additional sorting.

Follow the Bouncing Ball
Producing matching beginning sounds

With this circle-time game, students are sure to have a ball! Have little ones stand in a circle. Choose a volunteer to stand in the center of the circle and hold a large ball. The child says a beginning sound and bounces the ball to a classmate. The child who catches the ball names a word that begins with the chosen sound and then bounces the ball to another student who names a different word. Play continues in this manner for several rounds. To play again, choose another student to stand in the center and say a different beginning sound.

Can You Guess?
Blending phonemes

Everyone gets to join in with a circle-time guessing game! In advance, place in a bag several items whose names have three or four sounds. Decide on one object in the bag and sing the song to the class. At the end of the song, say the segmented name of the object. Encourage little ones to blend the sounds and name the object. When it is named correctly, invite a child to remove it from the bag. Repeat the activity until all items have been guessed.

(sung to the tune of "If You're Happy and You Know It")

Can you guess what I've got hidden in this bag?
Can you guess what I've got hidden in this bag?
If you listen for the word,
Tell me every sound you heard.
Then you'll know what I've got hidden in this bag!
/m/, /u/, /g/.

Stir It Up!
Blending phonemes

Mix some sound-blending practice with an imaginary blender! Cut out a copy of the picture cards on page 26 and place them in a pocket chart. Display a large blender cutout within students' reach. Secretly choose a pictured word and say the segmented sounds as you pretend to put each sound in the blender. Repeat the sounds as necessary and lead little ones in blending the sounds together to make the word. After the correct word is determined, have a child find the matching picture card and tape it to the blender. Repeat the activity with the remaining cards or until the blender is full.

/b/, /e/. Bee!

Mystery Word
Blending phonemes

Bring on the smiles with a cute puppet and this catchy tune! Use a puppet of your choice to sing the song. At the end of the verse, have the puppet say a familiar word in segments. Help students blend the sounds together and then say the word. Repeat the song with other words as time allows.

(sung to the tune of "The Farmer in the Dell")

Do you know my word?
Oh, do you know my word?
Put the parts together now,
And then you'll know my word!

/f/, /a/, /n/.

Fan.

/t/, /ī/. Tie.

Sound Train
Segmenting and blending phonemes

All aboard for this small-group activity! Make enough copies of the train workmat on page 26 for each child in the group plus one for yourself. Also cut out a copy of the picture cards on page 26. Give each child four counters and a workmat. Next, show youngsters a picture card and have them name it. Help little ones segment the sounds in the word. Demonstrate how to place a counter on each box on the workmat for each sound heard and then say the blended word. Encourage youngsters to segment and blend the word again before removing their counters. Repeat the activity with the remaining picture cards.

Sun.

Ssss-uuuu-nnnn.

Sun.

Stretch It Out
Segmenting and blending phonemes

For this class activity, show students an oversize rubber band and demonstrate how it stretches. Tell them they will be stretching words just as you're stretching the rubber band. Place the band around both hands with your palms facing each other and the band taut but not stretched. Say the word *rat* while holding your hands still. Now say *rat* again, but this time, stretch the sounds as you stretch the rubber band outward *(rrrr-aaaa-t)*. Then bring your hands back to the starting position and again say *rat.* Direct young-sters to hold their hands in front of them and pretend they each have a rubber band. Call out a word and have them say it, repeat it while stretching their pretend bands, and then bring their hands back together and say the word again.

Get Popping!
Segmenting and blending phonemes

To begin this circle-time game, read a word from the list shown. Lead little ones in segmenting the sounds of the word. Then ask them what sounds they hear at the beginning, middle, and end of the word. Next, choose three volunteers to squat in a row. Assign each child one of the sounds in the word. On your signal, have each youngster pop up, in turn, like popcorn as she says her sound. Then have the remaining youngsters announce the blended word. Repeat the activity with different words and different student volunteers.

/a/!

/p/!

/n/!

Pan!

pan	mop
mud	sit
cat	fun
run	ship

Gift Giving
Segmenting and blending phonemes

Here's a small-group activity that keeps on giving! To prepare, wrap a small gift box and lid separately so they look like a present. Place a cutout copy of the picture cards on page 26 facedown on a table. Invite a student to choose a card, silently identify the picture, and then place the card in the gift box. Next, have him give the gift to another child and tell her what is in the box by segmenting the word aloud. After the receiving student correctly identifies the word, ask her to open the box and remove the card. Then encourage her to prepare and give the next gift. Continue in the same manner until all the presents have been given.

/n/, /e/, /t/.

/m/
/a/
/n/

Suggested word pairs:

man, pan
pat, hat
hit, sit
hop, pop
bug, rug

win, tin
hen, pen
log, hog
wet, get
sun, fun

Man.

Switcheroo
Manipulating phonemes

Little ones are on the move with this sound-swapping game! Invite three youngsters to stand side by side. Assign each student a different sound of a CVC word. (See the suggested word pairs.) Instruct the youngsters to say their sounds in succession. Then encourage the class to blend the sounds and name the word. Next, have the student with the first sound sit down and invite a different child to take his place. Assign that student the beginning sound of the other word from the word pair. Have the three students say their sounds again and help the class blend the sounds together to make a new word. Repeat the activity with a different set of students for each listed pair of words.

Find tools for assessing phonological awareness on pages 31–34.

Rhyming Picture Cards

Use with "Roll It!" on page 5, "Partner Up" and "Ripe for the Picking" on page 6, and "Not Me!" on page 7.

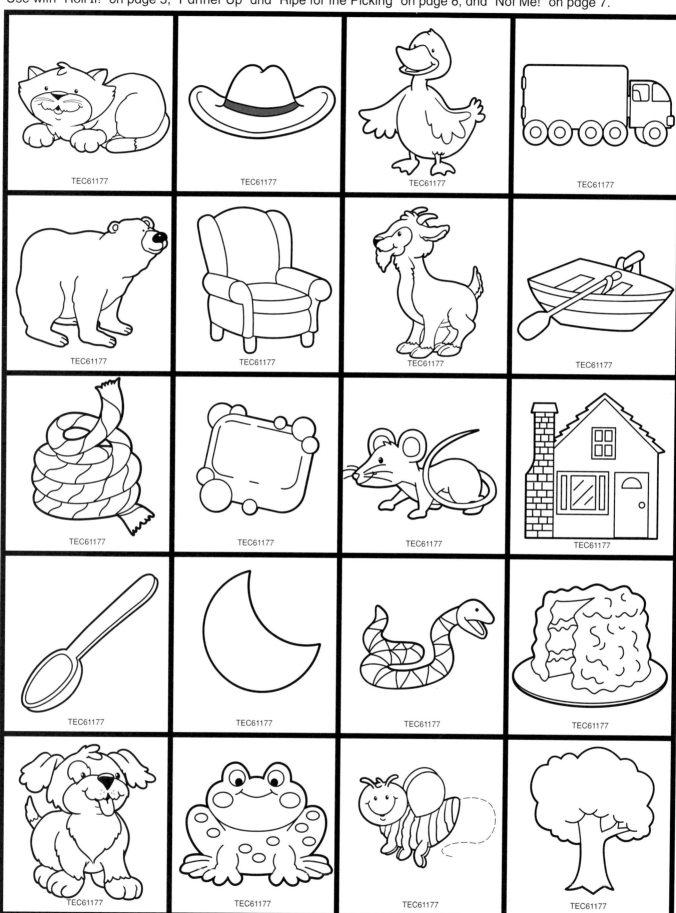

TEC61177   TEC61177   TEC61177   TEC61177

TEC61177   TEC61177   TEC61177   TEC61177

TEC61177   TEC61177   TEC61177   TEC61177

TEC61177   TEC61177   TEC61177   TEC61177

TEC61177   TEC61177   TEC61177   TEC61177

Almost Ready to Read • ©The Mailbox® Books • TEC61177

Did you ever see a

sitting on a  ?

Not me!

Almost Ready to Read • ©The Mailbox® Books • TEC61177

1

Did you ever see a

sailing a  ?

Not me!

2

Did you ever see a

driving a ☐ ?

Not me!

3

Did you ever see a

wearing a 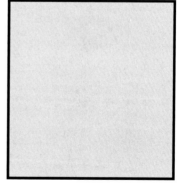 ?

Not me!

4

Food Cards

Use with "Higgledy-Piggledy" on page 7.

Caterpillar Card

Use with "Feeding Time!" on page 9.

Pig Pattern
Use with "Higgledy-Piggledy" on page 7 and
"Please Feed the Animals!" on page 13.

Cat Pattern
Use with "Please Feed the Animals!"
on page 13.

Camera Pattern
Use with "Say Cheese!" on page 13.

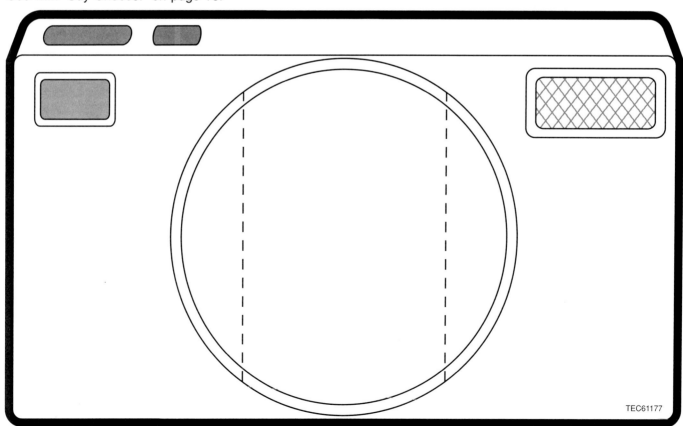

Almost Ready to Read • ©The Mailbox® Books • TEC61177

Picture Cards
Use with "Please Feed the Animals!" and "Say Cheese!" on page 13,
"Three-Ring Circus" on page 14, and "All Aboard!" on page 15.

TEC61177	TEC61177	TEC61177	TEC61177
TEC61177	TEC61177	TEC61177	TEC61177
TEC61177	TEC61177	TEC61177	TEC61177
TEC61177	TEC61177	TEC61177	TEC61177
TEC61177	TEC61177	TEC61177	TEC61177

Picture Cards

Use with "Stir It Up!" on page 16, "Sound Train" on page 17, and "Gift Giving" on page 19.

Train Workmat

Use with "Sound Train" on page 17.

Almost Ready to Read • ©The Mailbox® Books • TEC61177

Rhyme Time

🖍 Color the pictures that rhyme in each set.

Name_____

Matching beginning sounds

Monster's Munchies

 Cut.

 Glue to match the beginning sounds.

Almost Ready to Read • ©The Mailbox® Books • TEC61177

28

Name_____

Bunches of Balloons

 Cut.

Glue to match the ending sounds.

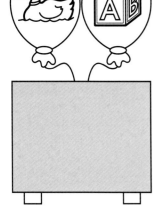

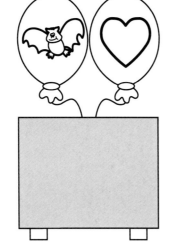

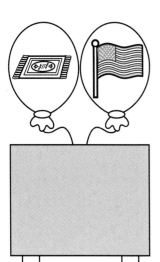

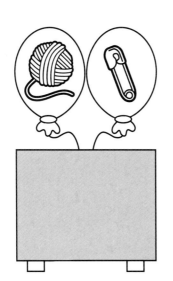

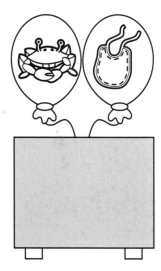

Almost Ready to Read • ©The Mailbox® Books • TEC61177

Say Those Sounds!

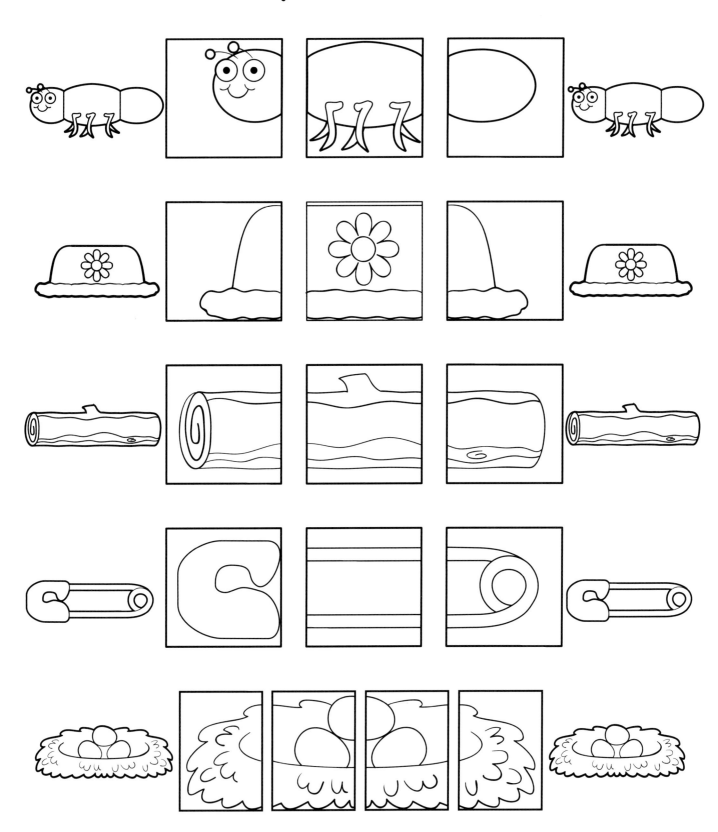

Almost Ready to Read • ©The Mailbox® Books • TEC61177

Note to the teacher: Have each student point to the first picture in the top row and say, "Bug." Then lead her to point to one box for each sound in the word. Have her point to the last picture in the row and repeat the word *bug.* Then have the child repeat each sound as she colors each box. Continue in this manner for the remaining rows.

Name _____

Date _____

Almost Ready to Read • ©The Mailbox® Books • TEC61177

Note to the teacher: Have each child point to the first row of pictures. Name each picture in the row. Ask the child to color two pictures that rhyme. Repeat with each remaining row of pictures.

31

Note to the teacher: Have each child point to the picture in the first box and name it. Then have her clap the word parts as she names the picture again. Direct her to color a circle for each word part. Repeat with each remaining box.

Name ______________________________

Date ______________________________

Informal Assessment

Matching beginning sounds

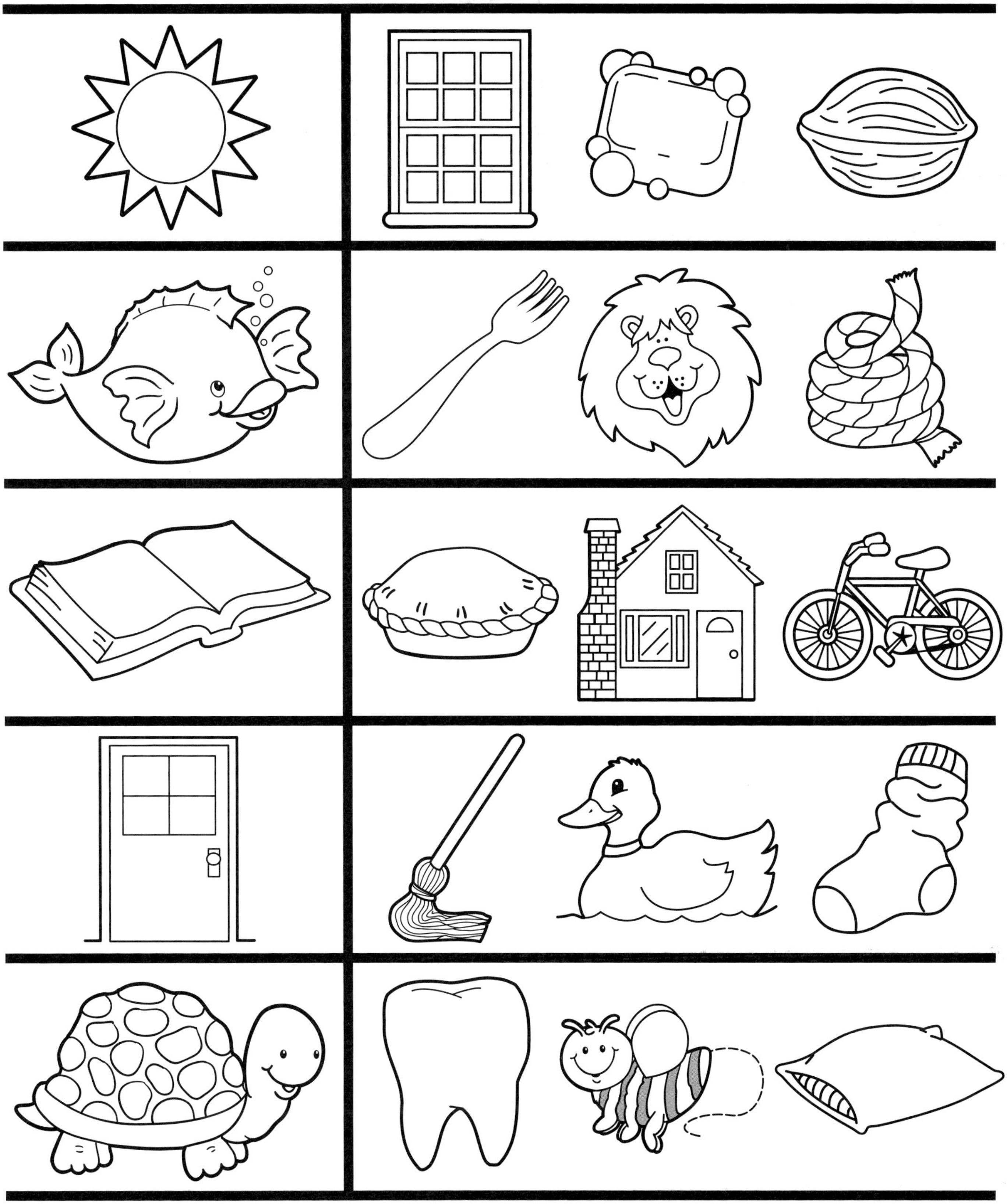

Note to the teacher: Have a child point to the first picture in a row and name it. Have the child name the remaining three pictures in the row. Ask the child to color the picture that has the same beginning sound as the first picture. Repeat with each remaining row of pictures.

Note to the teacher: Have a child name the picture in the first row. Then have her say the word slowly as she slides a counter into a box for each sound (phoneme) she hears. Record the number of counters to represent the number of phonemes she heard. Repeat with each remaining row.

Print Awareness

Strike a Pose!
Connecting spoken and written words

Get your camera ready for this smile-inducing idea! Provide a box of props, such as clothing and items from a dramatic-play center. Allow each child to select one or more items from the box to use in a pose. Using a digital camera, take a picture of each little one. Print the pictures and give each youngster her own picture. Have her dictate a sentence about her picture to you as you write it on a sentence strip. Read the sentence back to the child, reinforcing that you wrote exactly what she said. During circle time, invite each child to show her picture and help her read her sentence strip. Create a picture gallery by displaying the photos with their corresponding sentences.

I am going to put out a fire.

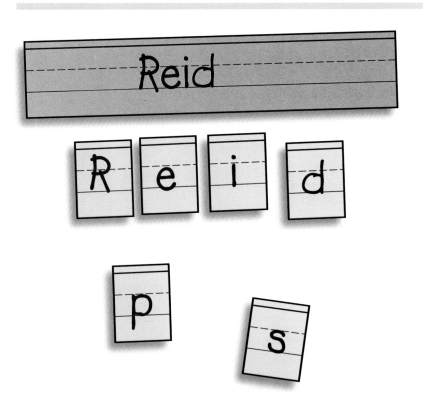

Personal Puzzles
Recognizing the letters in one's name

To prepare a puzzle for each child, write each student's name on a piece of a sentence strip. Then write each letter of his name on a separate small piece of a sentence strip and add two letters that are not in his name. Place each youngster's name card and letter cards in a resealable plastic bag. Give each child his bag and have him place his name strip on a table. Then encourage him to use the letter cards to match his name. If desired, add additional letter cards to make the activity more challenging.

Photo Gallery
Recognizing names

This picture-perfect daily attendance chart provides little ones with name recognition practice. In advance, write each child's name on a length of sentence strip. Place a photo of each child along the top of a pocket chart and the name cards along the bottom. Every morning, a child finds his name and places it next to his photo. After all students have arrived, look to see if any youngsters are absent. If so, ask a child to point to the name card of the missing student and read the name aloud. Then have students sing the song shown while the youngster continues to point to the name card.

(sung to the tune of "Pawpaw Patch")

Where, oh, where is sweet little [Karen]?
Where, oh, where is sweet little [Karen]?
Where, oh, where is sweet little [Karen]?
[She] is not at school today!

Scrambled Eggs
Recognizing names

Here's a fun circle-time game that promotes print awareness and boosts memory skills. For each child, label a copy of the egg pattern on page 45 with her name. During circle time, invite three youngsters to be eggs and stand in front of the group holding their personalized egg cutouts. Guide the class in reading each child's name aloud. Discuss characteristics of each name, such as the beginning letter, number of letters, or repeated letters. Next, have the seated students close their eyes and repeat the chant, "Scramble, eggs, scramble!" while you help the eggs switch names with each other. After the names are switched, direct the eggs to announce, "We're scrambled!" and have little ones open their eyes. Assist the class in reading the names and matching them to their owners.

Sign In, Please!
Recognizing and writing one's own name

Give little ones name-writing practice with this daily routine! Make several copies of the sign-in sheet on page 46. Program the first column with the names of students in the class. In the second column, either write the names again using dotted letters or leave it blank for students to write their own names. Place the sign-in sheets near the classroom door. Encourage each youngster to sign in every morning by finding her name on the list and either tracing over it or writing it in the second column. Periodically rearrange the order of the names on the list so that students have to look closely for their names.

What's on the Menu?
Purpose of print

Help little ones learn about practical uses of print while they order up some fun! Give each child a copy of the menu cards on page 47 and a 9" x 12" sheet of construction paper folded in half. Lead students in a discussion about what a menu is and times they have used one. Then explain that they will make menus for their own make-believe restaurants. Help each child cut out the menu cards, choose ten food items, and glue them to her paper to make a menu. Next, invite her to name her restaurant and decorate the front of her menu. Encourage little ones to take their menus home and read them to their families.

Everyday Reading
Purpose of print

Help youngsters appreciate that different printed materials are all around us and help us every day. Place in a basket a wide range of printed materials, such as maps, catalogs, magazines, newspapers, coupon flyers, menus, recipes, and books. Choose one or two items to discuss each day and then place the collection in your reading area so that little ones can explore the varieties of print on their own.

Special Delivery
Purpose of print

Set up a mailroom in your dramatic-play area! Label a supply of child-appropriate mail items—such as packages, letters, and magazines—with imaginary addresses, similar to the ones shown. Store the mail in a large container. Nearby, set up several shoeboxes labeled with addresses that match the mail. When a student visits the center, he pretends to be a mail carrier by choosing an item, matching the address to one of the mailboxes, and delivering it.

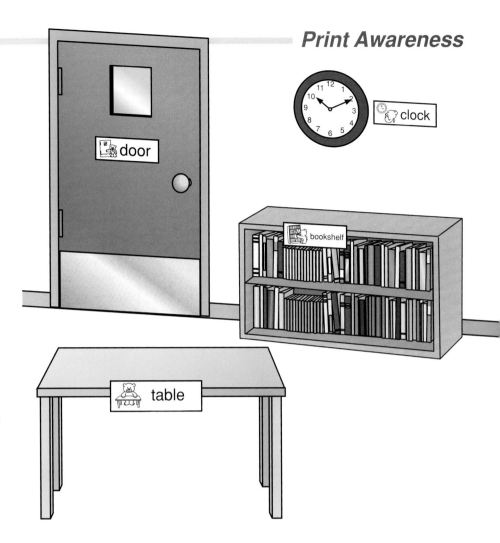

Lively Labels
Purpose of print

Enlist students' help in adding written words to everyday classroom items. Cut out a construction paper copy of the classroom labels on pages 48–50. During circle time, present a label and help students read it. Next, invite a child to locate the item that matches the label and assist him in posting the label near the item. During circle time the next day, ask the child to find his label and read it to the class. Then invite a different youngster to help you label another classroom item. Before long, students will be reading all around the room!

Product Pairs
Environmental print

For this center, collect matching pairs of empty, clean food containers. Store the containers in a toy grocery cart or shopping bags and place them in your dramatic-play area. When a student visits the center, she unloads the groceries and matches the pairs. For more advanced students, place at the center a grocery list with the names of selected food items. A student finds only the grocery pairs that are on the list.

Bag It!
Environmental print

With this idea, alphabet practice and product identification are in the bag! In advance, gather several empty, clean grocery containers on which each product's name begins with one of three different letters. Make three copies of the grocery bag pattern on page 51. Label each bag with a different letter to match the names of the gathered items. Then cut out the bags and post them in an open area. To begin, give a child an item. Help her identify the product name and beginning letter. Then encourage her to place the item near the matching bag. Continue in the same manner for each remaining item.

Read Around the School
Environmental print

What better way to practice reading than to feature words little ones see every day? Program a copy of the recording sheet on page 52 with words from familiar signs around your school; then copy to make a class supply. Help each child attach his paper to a clipboard or other writing surface. Then have youngsters take their clipboards and a crayon and lead them around the school to search for the signs that match their papers. When a youngster spots one of the signs on his sheet, he colors the box next to the word. After the tour is over, lead little ones in discussing their findings.

Handle With Care!
Book handling

Reward little ones for using proper book-handling techniques! Enlist students' help in demonstrating how to hold a book correctly, how to turn the pages carefully, and how to put books away after reading them. Then explain that it is important never to draw or write in a book and never to tear the pages. Teach little ones the song shown and then model the rules during a class read-aloud.

Send home with each student a copy of page 53. Instruct each youngster to read a book at home with a family member and color a box for each rule he follows. After each student returns his completed sheet, give him a copy of an award pattern on page 54.

Books Are Special
(sung to the tune of "Clementine")

Books are special, books are special,
And they need some special care.
We can learn to treat our books well.
Here are rules for us to share.

Hold the book or lay it down flat.
Turn the pages carefully.
Put it away when you're finished.
Treat a book respectfully!

Zoom!

The racecars are all in a line.

It is almost starting time.

On your mark, get set, go!

Zooming quickly, never slow!

Around the track at a fast pace.

Which car is going to win the race?

Here comes red, now orange and green.

Hooray! Blue's the fastest car we have seen!

Zooming Ahead!
Tracking print

Using a racecar pointer helps students track print in a poem. Color and cut out a construction paper copy of the racecar on page 45; then attach it to the end of a craft stick. Copy the poem shown onto chart paper and draw a flag at the end of each line. Show students the poem and pointer and explain that the racecar always drives toward the flag. Then use the racecar to track the print as you read the poem aloud. To reinforce the concept of return sweep, at the end of each line, encourage students to point out where the car needs to go next. After several readings, invite student volunteers, in turn, to "drive" the racecar as you reread the poem.

Mary had a little lamb.

Hear It, Move It
One-to-one correspondence

For this small-group activity, write each line of a familiar nursery rhyme or poem on a different sentence strip and place the strips in a pocket chart. Lead students in reading the poem aloud several times, pointing to each word you read. Next, remove one sentence strip from the chart and place it on a tabletop in front of the group. Help students read the sentence; invite a youngster to place a manipulative below each word as it is read. Repeat with other strips as time allows.

Making Bouquets
Sorting letters and words

Arranging flowers helps little ones differentiate between letters and words. Cut out several copies of the flower patterns on page 55; then label some with letters and some with words. Spread out the flowers on a table and post two large vase outlines, labeled as shown, nearby. Gather a small group of students at the table and lead them to notice that most words have two or more letters grouped together. Next, teach students the song shown. Then invite a child to take a flower, sing the song, and determine whether the flower shows a word or a letter. After the group verifies his response, help him glue the flower to the correct vase. Continue until each flower arrangement is complete.

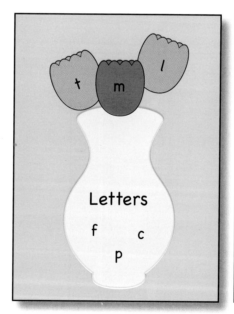

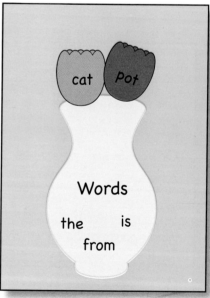

(sung to the tune of "London Bridge")

This one stands here all alone, all alone, all alone.
This one stands here all alone: It's a **letter.**

This has letters in a row, in a row, in a row.
This has letters in a row: It's a **word.**

Shapely Spaces
Spaces between words

To prepare, label each of several shape cutouts with one word from a sentence. Place the shapes word-side down in one row of a pocket chart with the shapes overlapping. Lead students to notice that it is hard to see the individual shapes because there is no space between them. Next, move the shapes so there is space between each one. Guide little ones to understand that because there is space between each shape, the shapes are easier to identify. Then repeat the activity with the word sides up. To connect this activity to reading, have students look through books to notice that there is space between all words in sentences.

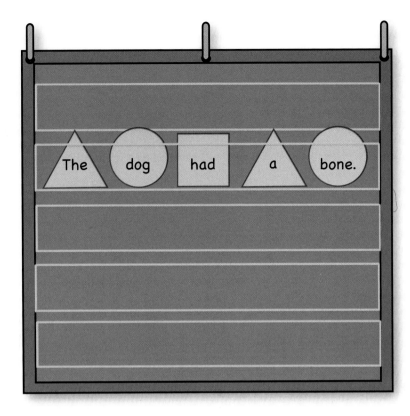

Point It Out
Concepts of print

For this group activity, review the different print concepts, such as identifying the front cover, the back cover, the title, the author, a letter, a word, a sentence, the first word on a page, and the last word on a page. Next, recite the first line of the chant shown. Then point to one of the book features and invite the class to reply by inserting the correct phrase in the second line of the chant. Continue in the same way, choosing a different feature each time.

Teacher: Look at the book, and what do you see?
Students: We see [the cover]. Yes sirree!

Oh no!

Oh No!
Concepts of print

Little ones act as the teacher when they correct your deliberate mistakes! Tell youngsters that as you read a big book aloud, they are to make sure you are reading the book correctly. Ask them to place their hands on their cheeks and say, "Oh no!" each time you make an error. To begin, place the book on the easel with the back cover facing out. After little ones correct you, continue by making other mistakes such as holding the book upside down, reading the last word on the page first, reading from right to left, or not stopping at periods. If desired, invite student volunteers to read the book to the class and make intentional mistakes.

The Dot Means Stop!
Basic punctuation

This catchy chant helps students understand the importance of ending punctuation. To prepare, write several sentence pairs on chart paper as shown. Read the first sentence pair, running the two sentences together without pausing. Ask the class whether you read correctly; then lead younsters to understand that you should have stopped between the two sentences. Next, lead youngsters in the chant shown. After reciting the chant, point to each word in the first sentence pair as you read it again. While reading, invite a child to draw periods in the correct locations. Continue with each remaining pair of sentences.

I have a cat Her name is Puff

Ben went to the park He rode his bike

My dad threw the ball It went far

We swam in the pool The water was cold

The dot means stop and take a break.
The dot means stop, for goodness' sake!
The dot means stop. The sentence is done.
Now start right in on the very next one!

Find a tool for assessing print awareness on pages 57–62.

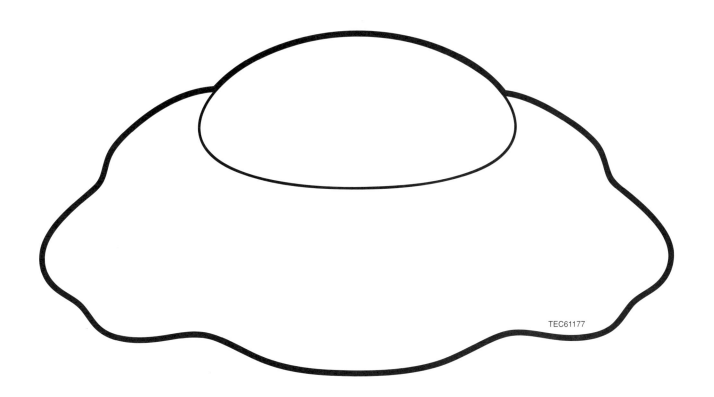

TEC61177

Racecar Pattern
Use with "Zooming Ahead!" on page 41.

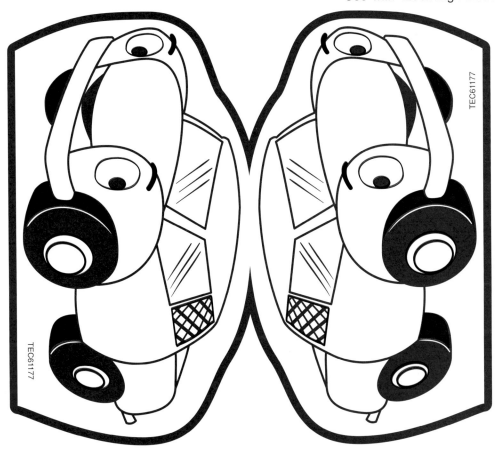

TEC61177

TEC61177

Welcome to _____'s Class!

Today is _____.

Sign in, please!

Almost Ready to Read • ©The Mailbox® Books • TEC61177

46   **Note to the teacher:** Use with "Sign In, Please!" on page 37.

chicken	hamburger
TEC61177	TEC61177
hot dog	pancakes
TEC61177	TEC61177
pasta	pizza
TEC61177	TEC61177
sandwich	taco
TEC61177	TEC61177
fruit	fries
TEC61177	TEC61177
chips	milk
TEC61177	TEC61177
juice	pie
TEC61177	TEC61177
ice cream	cake
TEC61177	TEC61177

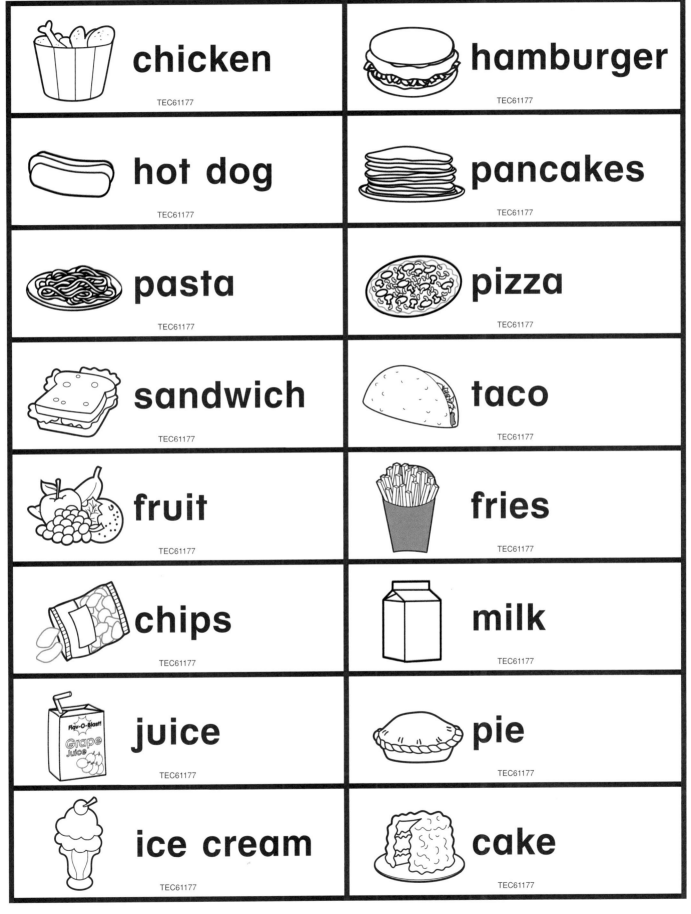

 window

TEC61177

 door

TEC61177

 sink

TEC61177

 clock

TEC61177

table

TEC61177

bookshelf

TEC61177

flag

TEC61177

desk

TEC61177

 computer

TEC61177

 board

TEC61177

calendar

TEC61177

 alphabet

TEC61177

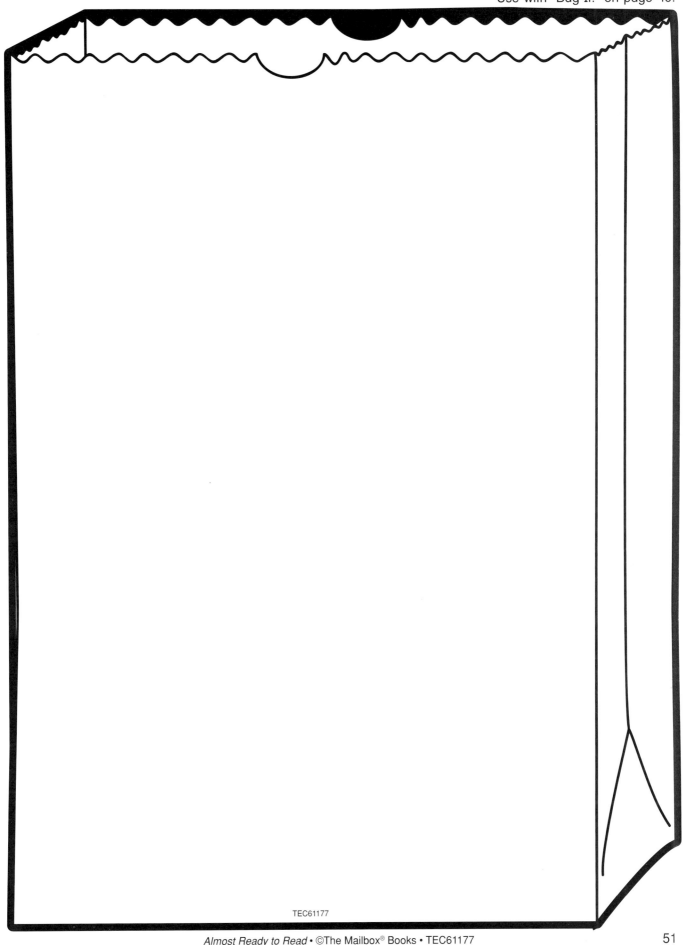

TEC61177

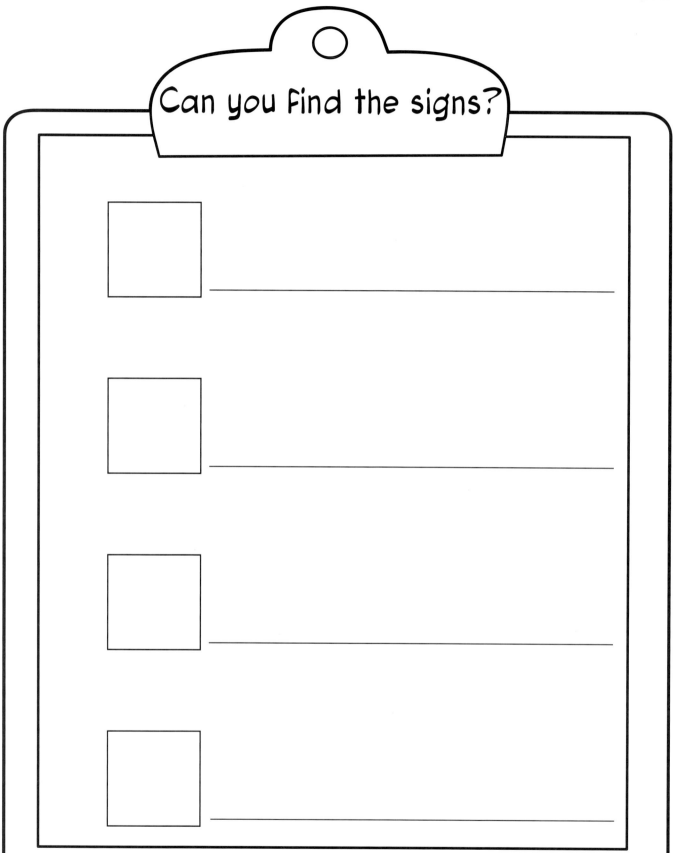

Can you find the signs?

Almost Ready to Read • ©The Mailbox® Books • TEC61177

Note to the teacher: Use with "Read Around the School" on page 40.

Handle With Care!

Always...

Hold your book upright or flat on a table.

Turn the pages carefully.

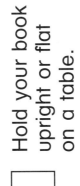

Put books away.

Never...

Write or draw in books.

Tear pages in books.

Almost Ready to Read • ©The Mailbox® Books • TEC61177

Note to the teacher: Use with "Handle With Care!" on page 41.

Award Patterns
Use with "Handle With Care!" on page 41.

_____
name

takes care of books!

TEC61177

TEC61177

takes care of books!
name

Almost Ready to Read • ©The Mailbox® Books • TEC61177

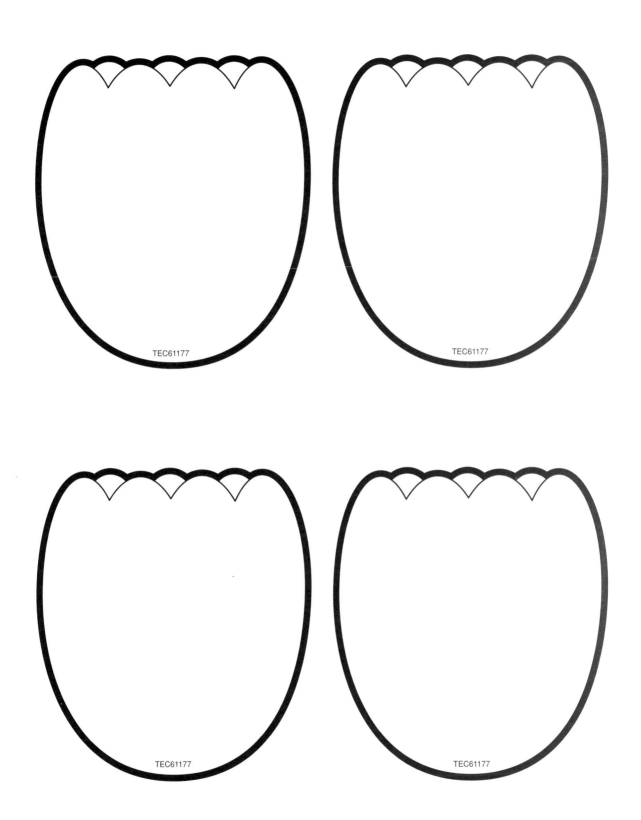

TEC61177

TEC61177

TEC61177

TEC61177

Peanuts for Sale

🖍 Color by the code.

Color Code

letter—blue
word—red

j man dog r

at s pet b

f sun v in

Print Awareness Assessment

To prepare, make one copy each of pages 58 through 62. Cut out the cover and booklet pages on the bold lines and color them if desired. Then fold the cover and booklet pages 2 through 8 on the thin lines, keeping the text and illustrations to the outside. Use a glue stick to seal the right edge and bottom of each folded page. Stack the pages in order behind the cover and then staple the stack on the left side to make a booklet. Make additional copies of the recording sheet on page 62 as needed.

To assess a child, follow the directions below and complete a copy of the recording sheet.

Cover
Skill: Can identify the front cover of a book
Directions: Hold the booklet by the right edge. Pass the booklet to the child and ask him to show you the front cover. Then read the title aloud.

Pages 2 and 3
Skills: Knows that print carries the message; knows where to start and stop reading
Directions: Instruct the child to show you where to start reading. After he responds, have him show you where to stop reading. Then read page 2 aloud.

Pages 4 and 5
Skills: Knows that a left-hand page is read before a right-hand page; distinguishes between letters and words
Directions: Ask the child to show you where to start reading. After he responds, read the pages aloud. Next, have him point out and name one or more letters he knows. Then ask him to show you any one word.

Pages 6 and 7
Skill: Runs finger over or below text from left to right
Directions: Instruct the child to point to the words as you slowly read them aloud.

Pages 8 and 9
Skill: Makes a return sweep
Directions: Ask the child to show you where to start reading and in which direction to read. Then instruct him to show you where to read next. After he responds, read page 8 aloud.

2

Wake up, Cow! Please come with me now.

Wake Up, Farm!

4

Wake up, Sheep! It is not time to sleep.

?

3

9

Wake up, Pig! The surprise is big.

Wake up, Pup! You must get up.

5

8

Hen has a new family!

Are you ready to come? Are you ready to see?

Wake up, Mouse! Come to the henhouse.

7

Almost Ready to Read • ©The Mailbox® Books • TEC61177

9

Name _____ Date _____

Print Awareness Recording Sheet

Booklet	Skills	Comments
Cover	• Front cover	
Pages 2 and 3	• Print carries the message • Where to start and stop	
Pages 4 and 5	• Left-hand page first • Letters and words	
Pages 6 and 7	• From left to right	
Pages 8 and 9	• Return sweep	

Almost Ready to Read • ©The Mailbox® Books • TEC61177

Letter Knowledge

Cherry Pies
Concept of letters

To prepare for this small-group game, make several copies of the cherry cards on page 79 and program them with different letters and nonletters. Place in your small-group area the cutout cards and two pie tins: one for students and the other for an imaginary opponent, such as a stuffed animal. To play, hold up a card. If the card shows a letter, a player places the cherry card in the students' pie tin; if it is not a letter, the opponent gets the cherry. The first pie to have ten cherries is declared the winner!

ABCs Afloat
Concept of letters

This supersize soup is reserved for letters only! Add to the water (soup) in your water table craft foam shapes, letters, and other symbols. Place a small plastic container on a corner of the table. Have youngsters use a slotted spoon to scoop all the nonletters out of the soup and set them in the container. For an added challenge, have students name each of the letters floating in the soup.

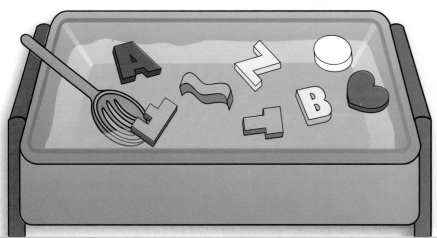

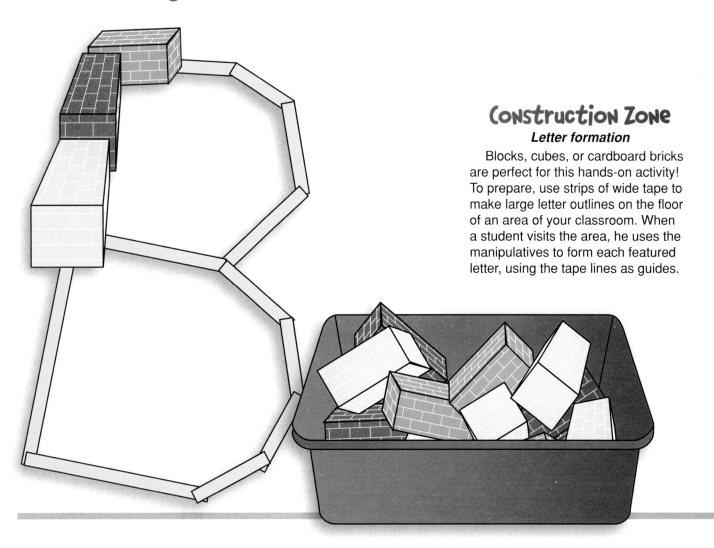

Construction Zone
Letter formation

Blocks, cubes, or cardboard bricks are perfect for this hands-on activity! To prepare, use strips of wide tape to make large letter outlines on the floor of an area of your classroom. When a student visits the area, he uses the manipulatives to form each featured letter, using the tape lines as guides.

Yarn Art
Letter formation

This interactive book is sure to be popular with your little ones! Glue a piece of felt on a sheet of cardstock for each letter of the alphabet. Program each prepared sheet with a different letter. Cut several lengths of yarn in different sizes and place them in a binder pouch. Store the pouch and the pages in a three-ring binder. To use the binder, a student removes the yarn from the bag and uses the letter headings as a guide to form desired letters on the felt.

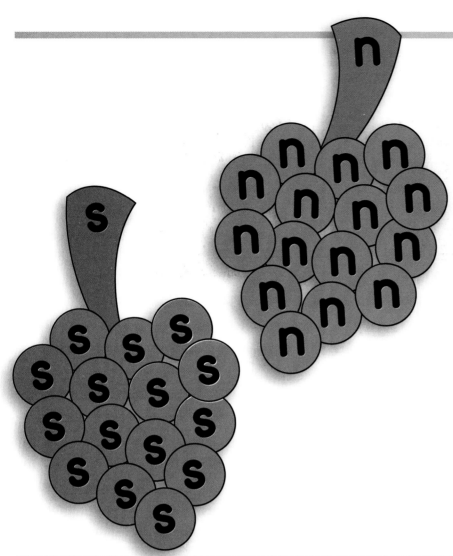

Bunches of Grapes
Matching letters

Everyone helps put these grapes into bunches! For an activity that's reprogrammable, laminate a half sheet of brown paper and several sheets of purple paper. Cut two stems from the brown paper and one circle per child from the purple paper. Use an erasable marker to program each cutout with one of two letters. During circle time, display the stems and give a circle to each child. Have each child, in turn, place his grape on the stem with the matching letter. Collect the cutouts for use at a center and then later reprogram them for another circle-time sorting activity.

Buzz!
Matching letters

For this honey of an activity, make a yellow copy of page 80 and three additional tan copies of the beehive cards on that page. Cut out the bee pattern and tape it to the end of a pointer. Program each yellow card with a different letter and then program three tan cards to match each yellow card. Cut out the cards and randomly display the tan cards and one yellow card in a pocket chart (or similar display). Point the pointer to the yellow card and make a buzzing noise. Then move the bee from hive to hive. Ask the youngsters to buzz each time the bee lands on a hive that matches the yellow one. Continue until the bee has visited each hive multiple times. On subsequent days, repeat the activity using different yellow cards.

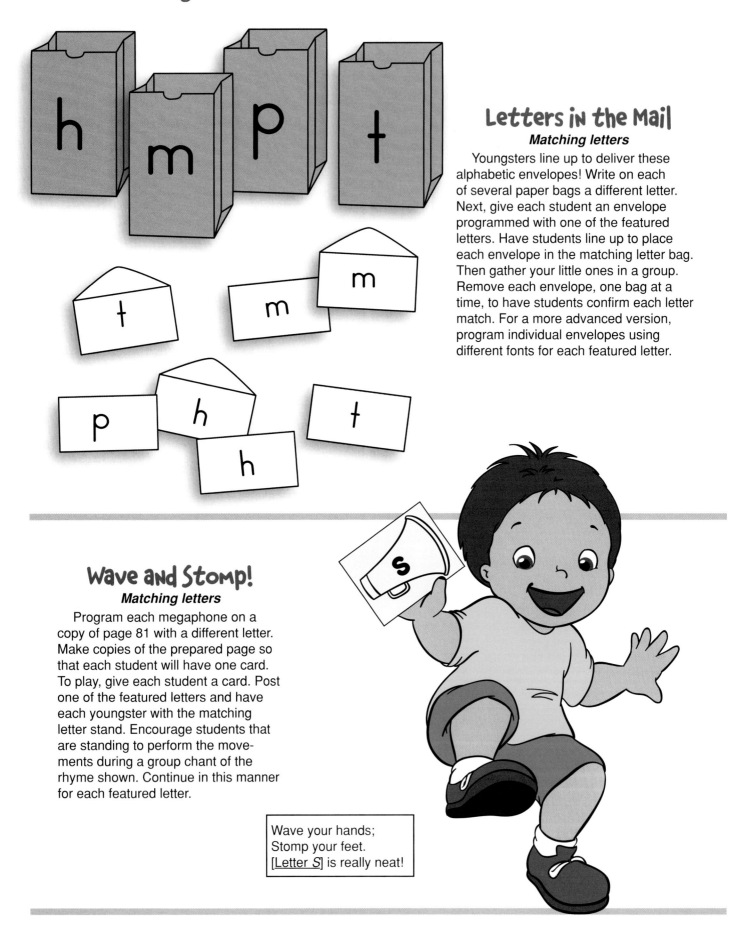

Letters in the Mail
Matching letters

Youngsters line up to deliver these alphabetic envelopes! Write on each of several paper bags a different letter. Next, give each student an envelope programmed with one of the featured letters. Have students line up to place each envelope in the matching letter bag. Then gather your little ones in a group. Remove each envelope, one bag at a time, to have students confirm each letter match. For a more advanced version, program individual envelopes using different fonts for each featured letter.

Wave and Stomp!
Matching letters

Program each megaphone on a copy of page 81 with a different letter. Make copies of the prepared page so that each student will have one card. To play, give each student a card. Post one of the featured letters and have each youngster with the matching letter stand. Encourage students that are standing to perform the movements during a group chant of the rhyme shown. Continue in this manner for each featured letter.

Wave your hands;
Stomp your feet.
[Letter *S*] is really neat!

Alphabet Tree
Matching letters

Students are sure to be eager to pick these apples! Make a copy of the apple patterns on page 82 for each letter you would like to feature. Write the same letter on each pair of apples. Cut out the apples and post them on a large tree cutout. Near the tree, place a basket. Then lead youngsters in chanting the poem. Invite volunteers, in turn, to find matching letters on a pair of apples and place them in the basket.

Way up high in the alphabet tree,
Two matching apples smiled at me!
Who can find a letter match
And place it in our apple batch?

Doggy Treats
Matching letters

For this small-group game, copy and cut out a supply of dog bone patterns from page 82. Write matching letters on each pair of bones. Gather your group and give each child two facedown dog bones. On your signal, each child turns the bones over and determines whether the letters match. If they match, the child barks like a dog. If they do not match, she does nothing. Collect the bones and redistribute them for another round.

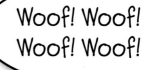

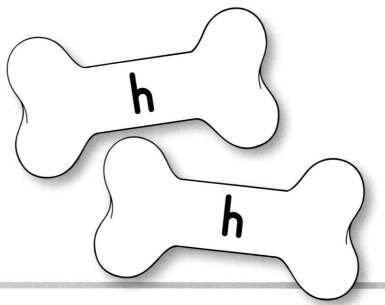

Butterflies in Motion
Matching letters

Fluttering butterflies and letter flowers make for an interactive class game! Write on each of several large flower cutouts a different letter. Program a class supply of cards with letters to match the flowers. To begin, post the flowers in open areas of your classroom. Then give each child a letter card and have her look around the room for the flower with the matching letter. On your signal, invite students to pretend to be butterflies and "fly" to the matching flower. After confirming each student's placement, collect the cards, redistribute them, and play again.

Wiggle Time!
Matching letters

Little ones get to boogie in their chairs with this lively class game! Prepare a 3 x 3 grid and program each space with a different letter. Give each child a copy of the grid to cut out; then have her shuffle the resulting cards and place them in a facedown stack. Also make a large set of matching letter cards for you to use. Display a letter card and then, on your signal, have each child flip over her top card. If the letter on her card matches the posted letter, she wiggles in her seat. If it does not match, she does nothing. After all the cards have been used, direct students to shuffle their cards to play again.

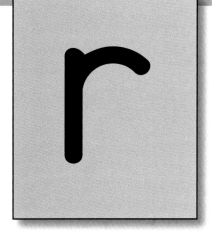

They match!

Many of the ideas in this section can easily be adapted to reinforce uppercase and lowercase letter matching.

Search and Find
Recognizing letters

Clipping letters out of magazines is sure to be a hit with your youngsters. Place three decorative bags, each labeled with a different letter, and used magazines at a center. When a student visits the center, he looks through the magazines for the letters shown on the bags. Each time he finds a matching letter, he cuts it out and drops it in the corresponding bag.

Cave Bears
Recognizing letters

Here's an at-a-glance activity to help you assess students' ability to recognize specific letters. Program each of the bear cards on a copy of page 83 with a different letter; then make a class supply of the page. Help each student cut out her copy of the bear cards and cave pattern. Then sing the song shown as each student places the corresponding bear on her cave. After singing the song, check for accuracy and then encourage each youngster to move her bear under her cave to pretend the bear is sleeping. Continue in this manner until each letter has been identified.

(sung to the tune of "Ten Little Indians")

Find the [*L*] bear and put it on the cave.
Find the [*L*] bear and put it on the cave.
Find the [*L*] bear and put it on the cave.
Then [*L*] bear will go to sleep!

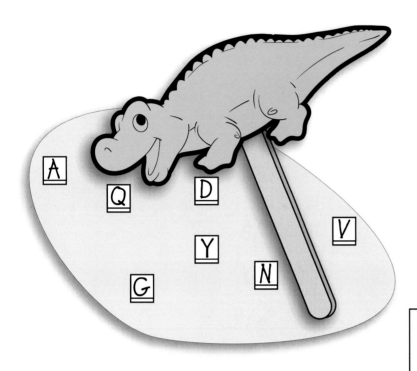

Sneaky Alligator
Recognizing letters

Heighten interest in your letter study with this small-group activity. Cut out a copy of the alligator patterns on page 84. Glue a large craft stick to the back of each cutout to make Mr. and Ms. Alligator puppets. Place several letter tiles on a large pond cutout. Give a group member an alligator puppet to play the part of Mr. or Ms. Alligator. Lead the group in the song shown, naming a letter in the pond where indicated. At the end of the verse, Mr. Alligator uses his hand to "snap" up the designated letter. Continue with more rounds until each youngster has played the part of Mr. or Ms. Alligator.

(sung to the tune of "Five Little Monkeys")

Look at all the letters swimming in the sea.
One little letter says, "Can't catch me!"
Along comes [Mr./Ms.] Alligator, quiet as can be,
And snaps letter [Q] right out of the sea.

Moon Mission!
Recognizing letters

For each member in your small group, program a copy of a spaceship from page 85 with a different letter. Place a moon cutout in your workspace to represent the creatures' home and give each child a spaceship. Announce one of the programmed letters. The child with the matching letter "flies" her spaceship to the moon. Continue in this manner until each group member has successfully completed a mission!

Hopper!
Recognizing letters

Students hop to letters for this whole-group activity! Cut out lily pads so there is one less than the number of students in your class. Write a different letter on each lily pad. Gather students in a circle, and invite one student to be the frog and sit in the center of the circle. Have each child in the circle place a lily pad in front of her, with the letter facing toward the frog. Next, students sing the alphabet song until you say, "Stop!" (Be sure to always stop when they sing a letter name programmed on a lily pad.) Then the frog hops to the lily pad with the corresponding letter and switches roles with the student sitting by it. Continue with more rounds as time permits.

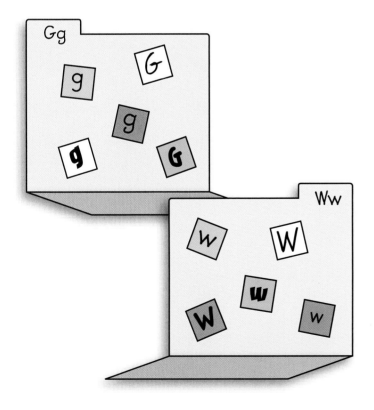

Fun With Fonts
Letter review

Create several ready-to-go activities with these letter files. Label one file folder for each letter of the alphabet. Inside each letter folder, insert a collection of different fonts of the same letter. Letters may be gathered from clip art, magazines, circulars, advertisements, coupons, and newspapers. Then see the suggestions below for fun ways to use these folders, or try a few ideas of your own!

Letter sort: Shuffle the contents of two letter files and have youngsters sort the letters into the corresponding folders.

Letter recognition: Glue on a sheet of construction paper several different letter fonts for several different letters. Name a letter and have students point to a matching letter.

Letter sequencing: Pull out one letter from each file folder and place the collection at a center. A youngster lines up the letters in alphabetical order.

Wyatt

Popular Pages
Naming letters

This class name book results in a photographic letter review. Take a photograph of each youngster holding a large poster of the first letter in his name. Glue the photo on a sheet of paper and write the child's name below it. Bind the completed pages into a class book for your reading area. Have youngsters work in pairs, with a volunteer, or in small groups to identify the featured letter on each page. For a more advanced version, write a complete sentence under each photo, such as, "*W* is for Wyatt."

Letter Detectives
Naming letters

Your little letter detectives will be on the move with this interactive idea. For each student, cut out the center of a construction paper circle and tape the circle to a craft stick so it resembles a magnifying glass. Also post different letters around the room. To begin, give each youngster a prepared magnifying glass and encourage her to search the room to find a letter. When she does, she says, "Aha!" and holds her magnifying glass in the air. After an adult confirms she can name the letter correctly, she proceeds to hunt for a different letter.

Aha!

Children! Children!
Naming letters

This variation on Eric Carle's book *Brown Bear, Brown Bear, What Do You See?* is sure to be a hit! Invite a youngster to play the role of the teacher and give her a pointer. Have her stand by your classroom alphabet, point to a letter, and ask, "Children, children, what do you see?" The class replies by inserting the correct letter into their response, saying, "We see the letter [S] looking at us!" To continue, invite a different youngster to be the teacher for another round. For an easier version, post fewer letters in your group-time area for students to identify.

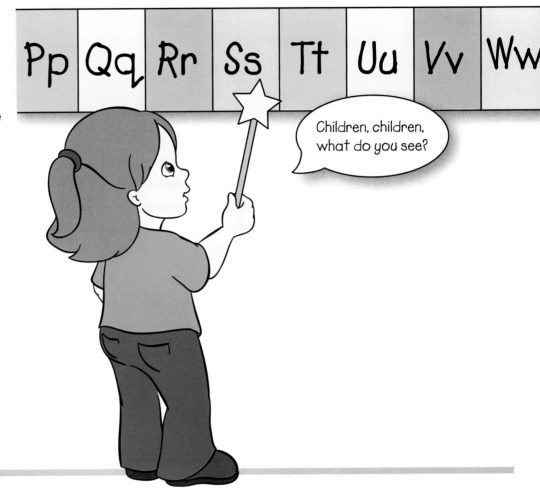

Pp Qq Rr Ss Tt Uu Vv Ww

Children, children, what do you see?

Please Find My Spots!
Naming letters

How can little ones help this dalmatian find his spots? By naming letters! To prepare, write different letters on a copy of the dog pattern on page 86. Post the prepared dog within students' reach and place a supply of black construction paper circles (spots) nearby. Encourage each child, in turn, to name a letter. After she correctly names a letter, invite her to tape a spot over the letter. This pooch will have his spots in no time!

Gumdrops, gumdrops,
Passed around.
Name the letter
That you found!

Goody Goody Gumdrops!
Naming letters

Students will cheer when letters are named correctly in this whole-group game. Write individual letters on a class supply of gumdrop cutouts and store them in a basket. To play, have youngsters sit in a circle and pass the basket around as you lead them in chanting the rhyme shown. At the end of the rhyme, the student holding the basket removes a gumdrop and announces the letter shown. If he is incorrect, help him to correctly name the letter. If he is correct, lead youngsters to say, "Goody goody gumdrops!" Continue in this manner with more rounds as time permits.

Build a Name
Naming letters

To make a book for each student, place between construction paper covers a blank sheet of paper for each letter in a child's name plus one more. Secure a photograph of the student on the front cover with her name. On the first page of the book, write the first letter in her name. Then, on the second page, write the first two letters in her name. Continue in this manner until the name is spelled in full. Then write the child's full name again at the bottom of the last page and have her draw a self-portrait. To review, read aloud different students' books for lots of engaging letter-naming practice.

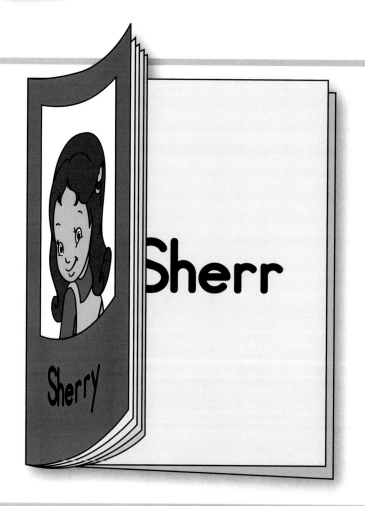

Tickets, Please!
Naming letters

There's no doubt students will be excited to get aboard this class train! Make a class supply of the ticket patterns on page 87. Write on each ticket a different letter and give one to each student. Have youngsters line up to pretend they are boarding a train. To get aboard, each child must identify the letter on her ticket. When all the passengers are aboard, lead them on a pretend train ride around the room.

A Fresh Batch
Naming letters

For this small-group activity, label cookie cutouts with different letters and place them on a baking sheet. Place in your small-group area the same number of bear counters as cookies. Invite youngsters, in turn, to name the letter on a cookie. Each time a letter is identified correctly, the child uses a spatula to serve a bear a cookie. When all the cookies have been served, consider offering a fresh batch of cookies to serve the bears a second helping!

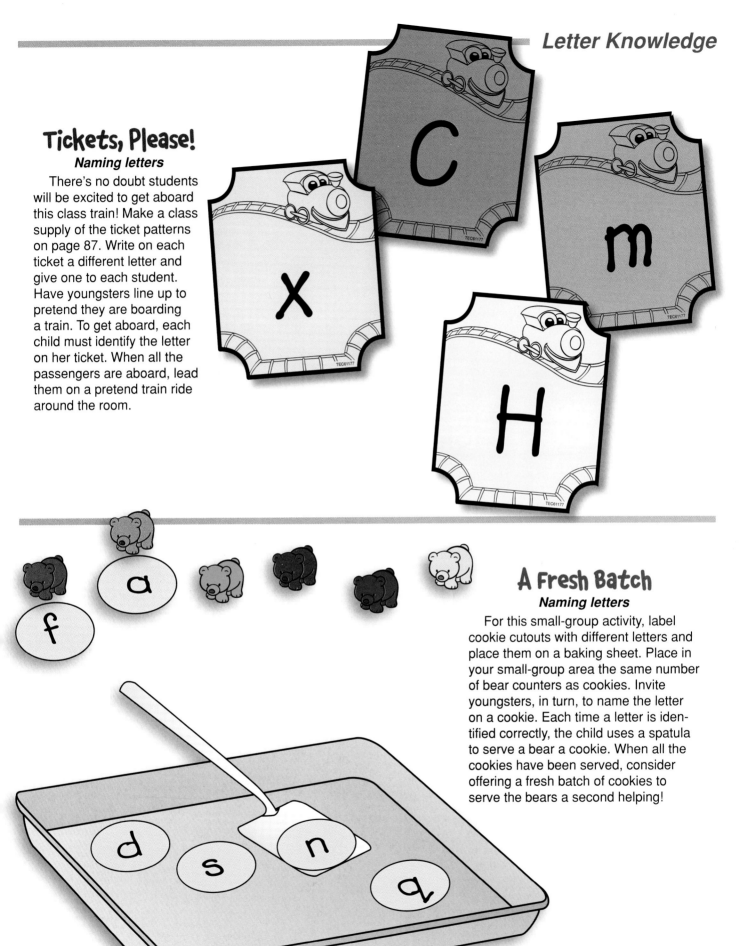

Letter Knowledge

Two Tall Towers
Naming letters

Students' name cards create a whole-group graphing activity that's easy to adapt for any letter! Post the uppercase and lowercase forms of a selected letter and have little ones name the letter. In a pocket chart, place "Yes" and "No" labels as shown. Next, hold up a name card and have youngsters look to see if it has the featured letter. Then read the student's name and have him place his name card in the corresponding column to show whether his name does or does not have the featured letter. Students are sure to be eager to find out which tower will be taller as each name card is added to the graph!

From A to Z
Naming letters

Students search for every letter in the alphabet to make this sequential strip. Provide materials such as magazines, circulars, advertisements, coupons, and newspapers from which youngsters can cut out letters. To make an alphabet strip, a child cuts out an *A* and glues it on the left side of a long paper strip. Then she searches for the letter *B,* cuts it out, and glues it next to the *A.* She continues in this manner, singing the "Alphabet Song" as a guide, until she has made her own alphabet strip from *A* to *Z.* When complete, encourage each child to point to each letter as she names it.

Forward and Back
Distinguishing letters

Youngsters are on the move with this whole-group game! Write a desired letter on ten large cards and different letters on several more cards. Post the featured letter and mark a starting line and finish line in your group-time area. To play, have youngsters line up along the starting line and name the posted letter. Then hold up a letter card and have them name the letter. If the featured letter is on the card, little ones hop forward one time. If the letter is not on the card, they hop backward one time. Play continues until all players have crossed the finish line.

Feed Me!
Distinguishing letters

This little letter monster is sure to be fed during this center activity. Program a copy of the monster pattern on page 88 with a desired letter. Then prepare different letter cards, being sure to include the featured letter several times. Place the cards and monster at a center. A child names the letter on each card and, in turn, compares it to the letter on the monster. If the letter on the card is not the letter on the monster, she sets the card aside. If the letters are the same, she pretends to feed the card to the monster!

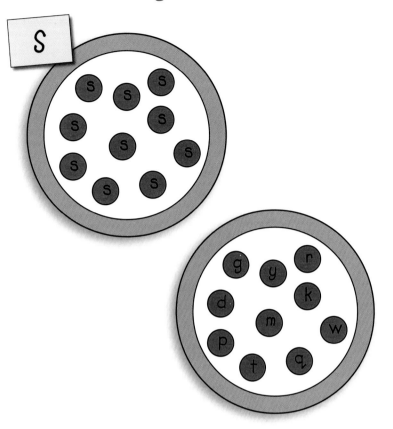

Pepperoni Pizza
Distinguishing letters

Pizzas are made to order at this center! Cut out and color two large circles so they resemble pizzas and label one of them with a desired letter. Write on each of several red circle cutouts (pepperoni) different letters, taking care to include several pieces with the featured letter. Place the prepared pepperoni and pizzas at a center. When a child visits the center, he names the letter on the programmed pizza. Then he takes one piece of pepperoni; names the letter; and, if it is the featured letter, puts it on the labeled pizza. If it is not the featured letter, he places it on the other pie. He continues in this manner until each pizza is made to order.

What a Catch!
Distinguishing letters

Reel in letter work with this class fishing game. Program several copies of the fish patterns on page 87 with a featured letter and program some with different letters. In your group area, place the fish facedown on a pond cutout along with a pail labeled with the featured letter. To begin, have a youngster pretend to go fishing and remove a fish from the pond. Encourage him to name the letters on the fish and the pail. If the letters are the same, he places the fish in the bucket. If the letters are different, he places the fish back on the pond. Continue in this manner until each child has had a turn to "fish."

Find tools for assessing letter knowledge on pages 93–96.

TEC61177

TEC61177

TEC61177

TEC61177

TEC61177

TEC61177

Bee Pattern and Beehive Cards
Use with "Buzz!" on page 65.

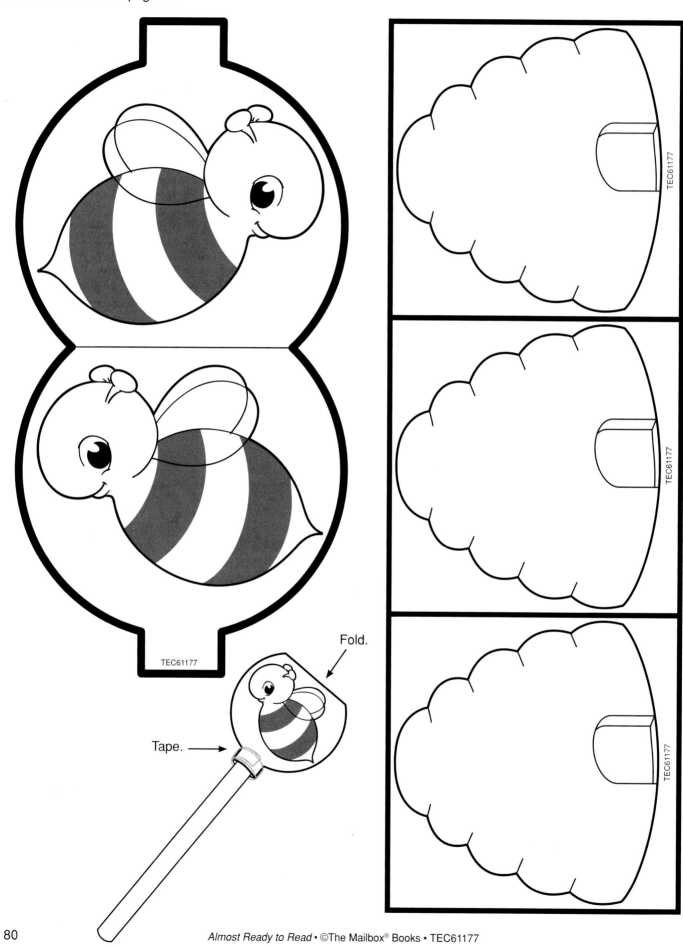

Fold.

Tape.

TEC61177

TEC61177

TEC61177

TEC61177

Almost Ready to Read • ©The Mailbox® Books • TEC61177

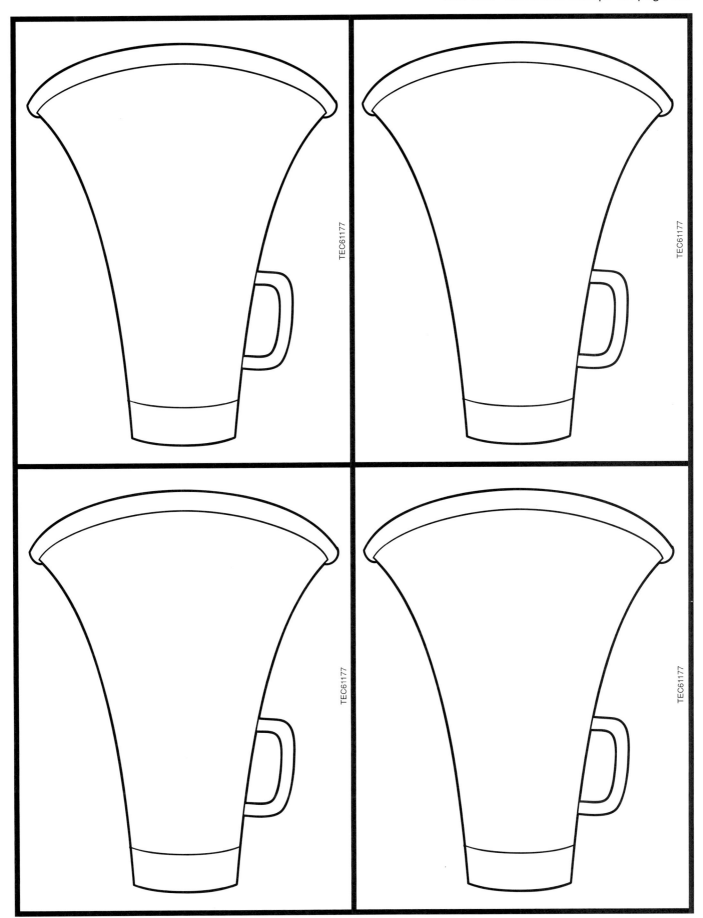

TEC61177

TEC61177

TEC61177

TEC61177

Apple Patterns
Use with "Alphabet Tree" on page 67.

TEC61177

TEC61177

Dog Bone Patterns
Use with "Doggy Treats" on page 67.

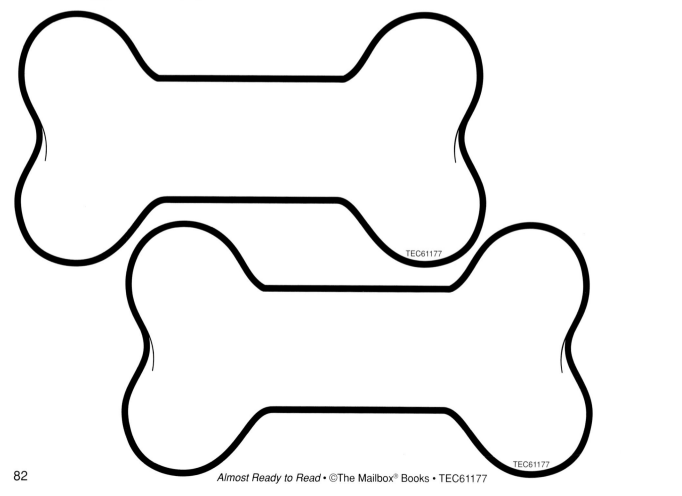

TEC61177

TEC61177

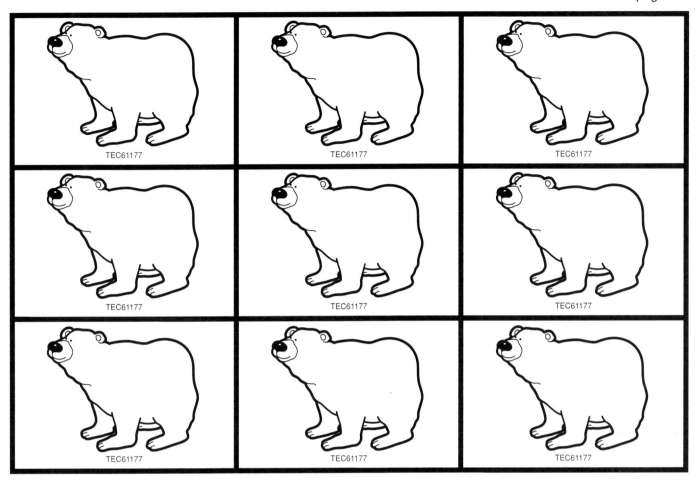

TEC61177

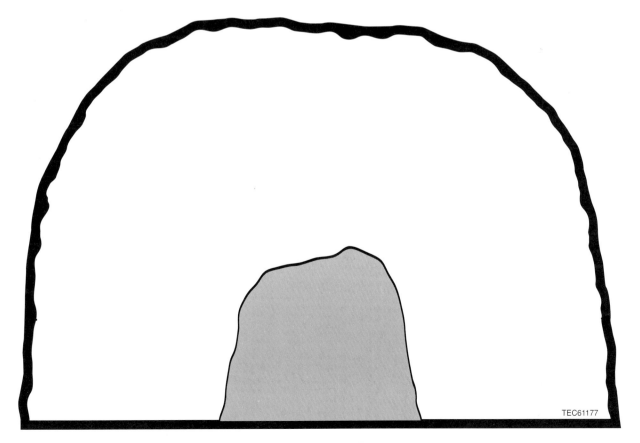

TEC61177

Alligator Patterns
Use with "Sneaky Alligator" on page 70.

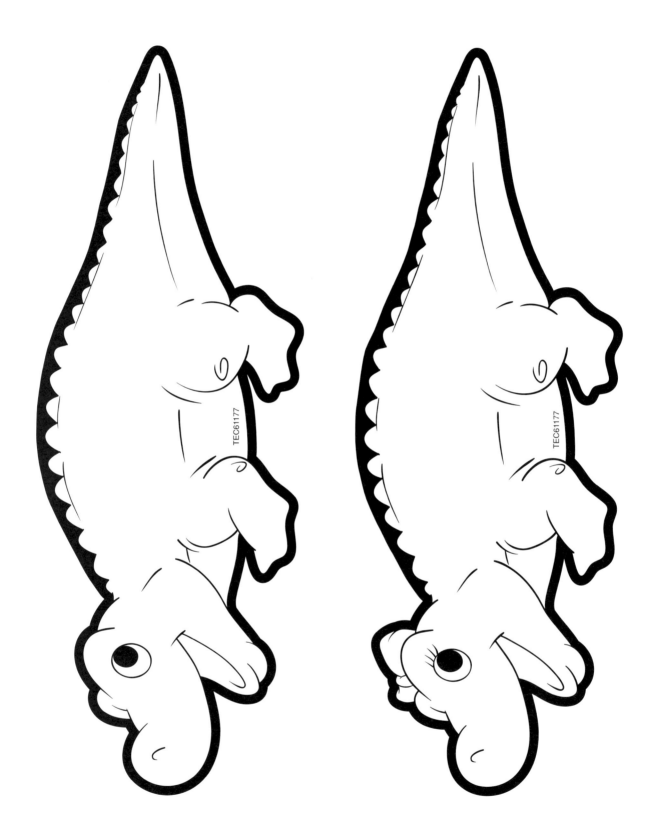

TEC61177

TEC61177

TEC61177

TEC61177

TEC61177

TEC61177

Dog Pattern
Use with "Please Find My Spots!" on page 73.

Almost Ready to Read • ©The Mailbox® Books • TEC61177

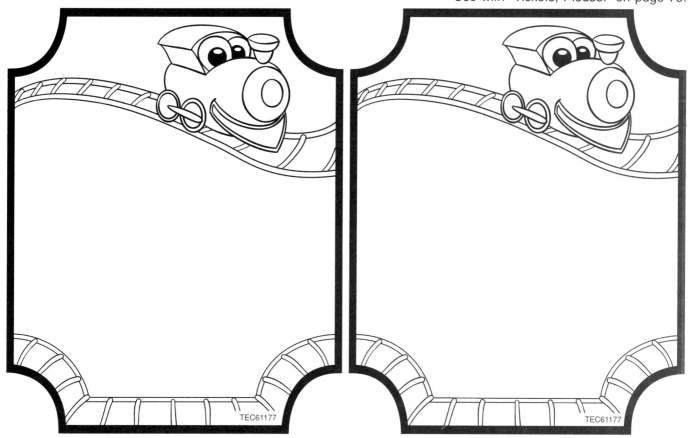

TEC61177

TEC61177

Fish Patterns
Use with "What a Catch!" on page 78.

TEC61177

TEC61177

Monster Pattern
Use with "Feed Me!" on page 77.

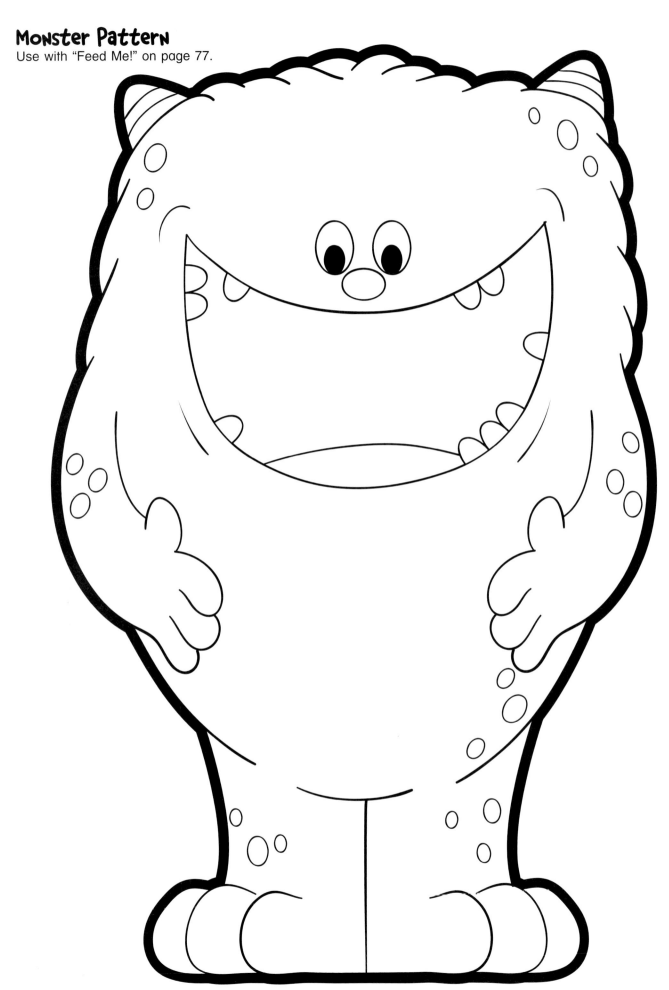

Almost Ready to Read • ©The Mailbox® Books • TEC61177

Name _____

Books! Books! Books!

✂ Cut. Sort.

🪣 Glue.

Letters A B C

Not letters ■ ▲ 〰

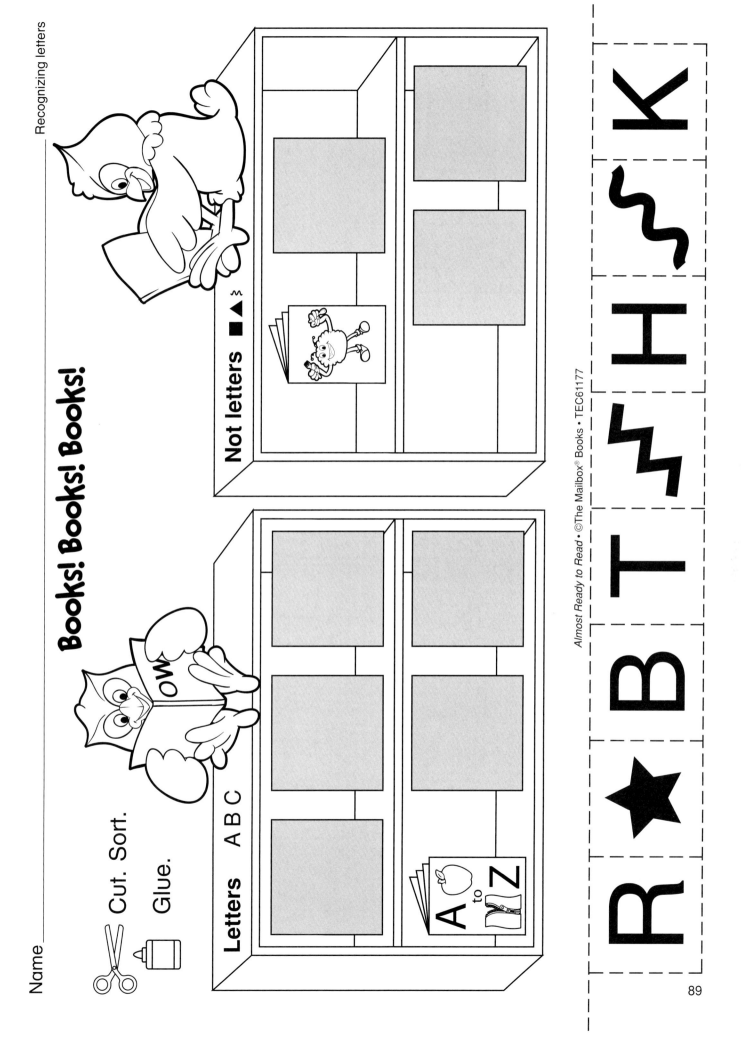

R ★ B T H 〰 〰 K

Strike!

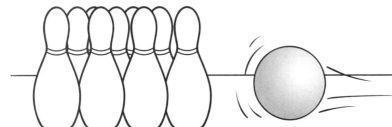

Color the matching letters in each set.

M	B	M	J	X	X
D	D	U	L	N	L
Z	A	Z	G	O	O
Q	S	S	F	F	W
T	E	E	R	C	R

Mmmm, Mmmm, Good!

 Color the matching letters
on each ice cream cone.

a
a
m

x
r
r

h
p
h

g
w
w

k
e
k

n
n
z

l
d
d

t
u
t

At the Pond

Color each 🐢 that has partner letters.

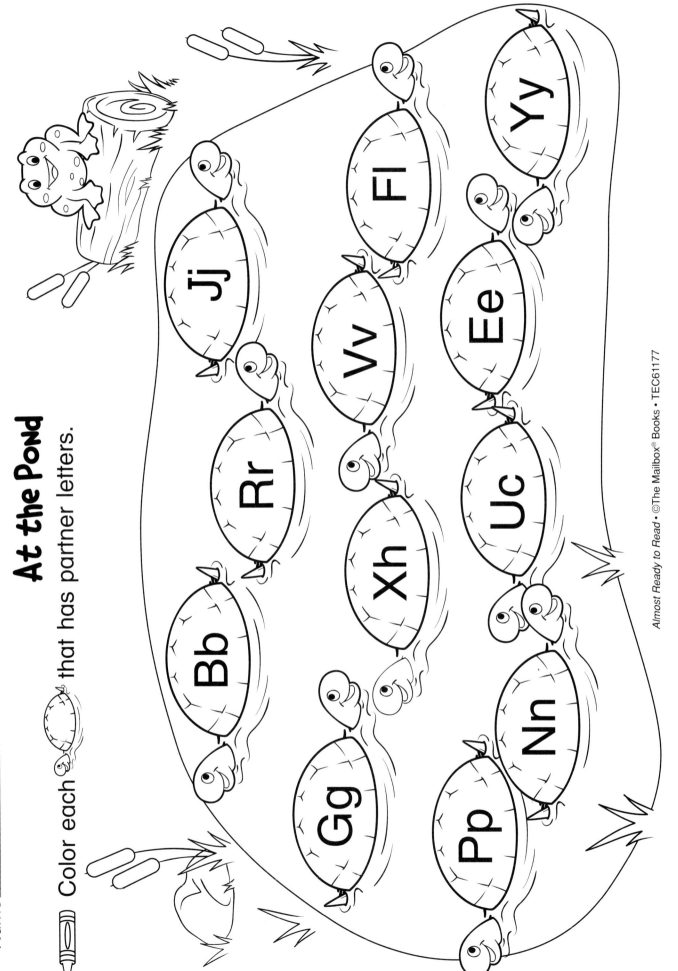

Name _____

Date _____

Informal
Assessment
Recognizing
letters

☀	 A	R	W	🍎	 M	T	O
🚣	 B	F	Y	🐟	 P	S	N
🌳	 U	C	H	🌙	 D	L	K
🏠	 r	x	p	🎈	 e	q	n
🌻	 m	g	l	🪁	 h	z	a
🛒	 j	v	f	⭐	 b	i	s

Almost Ready to Read • ©The Mailbox® Books • TEC61177

Note to the teacher: Prior to student use, make a master copy by circling one letter in each set. Then give each student an unmarked copy and have him find the set with the sun picture. Announce the circled letter on your copy and ask students to circle it on their papers. Continue for each remaining set. Repeat as desired to assess other letters.

Name ________________________________

Date ________________________________

Informal Assessment

Naming uppercase letters

F	K	P	O	V	B
Q	A	S	C	M	R
T	Y	G	D	N	E
H	X	U	L	Z	J
W	I				

Observations:

Note to the teacher: Personalize a class supply of this page plus one more. Using the extra copy, have a child name each letter. On the child's personalized page, circle each letter named incorrectly and record your observations.

Name ____________________

Date ____________________

Informal Assessment

Naming lowercase letters

c	t	m	p	r	w
h	b	i	l	g	a
u	z	j	x	d	o
f	q	e	n	v	k
y	s				

Observations:

Note to the teacher: Personalize a class supply of this page plus one more. Using the extra copy, have a child name each letter. On the child's personalized page, circle each letter named incorrectly and record your observations.

Name _____

Date _____

🖍 Color each box that has the correct partner letters.

Ss	Tk	Aa	Mm
Gg	Vv	Rr	Cc
Fh	Bb	Pg	Ii
Yy	Xf	Ww	Qq
Nn	Ee	Jj	Dz
Pp	Ll	Ko	Uu

Almost Ready to Read • ©The Mailbox® Books • TEC61177